The Handbook of Golf History

by
Dr. Douglas Lonnstrom
Professor of Statistics, Siena College

CO-AUTHOR
Sara Riso
Summer Scholar, Siena College

DORRANCE
PUBLISHING CO
EST. 1920
PITTSBURGH, PENNSYLVANIA 15238

Dorrance Publishing Co
585 Alpha Drive
Pittsburgh, PA 15238
Visit our website at *www.dorrancebookstore.com*

ISBN: 978-1-4809-6028-2
eISBN: 978-1-4809-6051-0

TABLE OF CONTENTS

GENE SARAZEN was one of the world's top players in the 1920's and

1930's. He was the first and is one of the five golfers (along with Ben Hogan, Gary Player, Jack Nicklaus and Tiger Woods) to win all current major championships in his career. Called the Career Grand Slam, Sarazen won the US Open in 1922, 1932; PGA Championship in 1922,1923 and 1933; the US Open Championship in 1932; the Masters Tournament in 1935. In addition, he invented the modern sand wedge, which changed the way professional golf was played and golf courses were designed.

Sarazen was also a philanthropist and leant his name to raise funds for numerous charities throughout the country and around the globe. One such charity was Siena College (www.Siena .edu) in Loudonville (Albany), New York where Gene and his wife, Mary, provided transformational support for the Gene and Mary Scholarship Fund at the national, liberal arts college, where Gene was awarded an Honorary Degree in 1978.

Following his degree ceremony, the Sarazens' set up a permanent way to provide scholahips for Siena College students. Students who "reflected the high personal, athletic, and intellectual ideals" of Gene and Mary, were granted financial awards to assist in their education. In the inaugural year, $100,000 was raised/donated to establish the initial endowment. Today that endowment stands at over $2.5 million and support 23 "Sarazen Scholars" with four-year educational scholarships. Through these scholars the Sarazen dream lives on, and will, in perpetuity.

Chapter 1:
GOLF HISTORY FOREWORD

HANDBOOK OF GOLF HISTORY

This book is intended to be a reference book featuring highlights of golf history. It is not intended to be a detailed history of golf; there are many great books that do that for certain time periods, equipment, courses, and players. However, if you want to look up the highlights of the 1800's or what happened in the year 1920, this is the book for you.

We give a summary of events leading up to the time of golf as we know it, what happened in the early centuries of golf (1400 to 1900), and then the major events from 1860 (creation of the OPEN championship) forward.

Frankly, as we delve into the early history of golf, it is difficult to be accurate. We have researched many sources, and they often do not agree. They may have different dates and names for the same event. As a result, we have used approximate dates where appropriate. As an example, the Haskell ball was invented in 1898, but we use 1900 because it is easier for the reader to place in context. Also, things do not happen overnight, so there is an overlap when in transition. The Haskell ball replaced the Gutta-percha, but not instantly, it took time. Same for metal woods, there are still players who use the wooden clubs.

WHO INVENTED GOLF?

The answer: NO ONE. Golf was not invented. It was not as if one day there was no golf and the next day, the game was created. Golf evolved over thousands of years from hundreds of stick and ball games. Probably the first forerunner of golf was bored shepherds in the fields thousands of years ago who took a stick and hit a rock into a gopher hole.

From there the idea just kept growing. The ancient Greeks, who are well-known to have had a huge impact on the history of many sporting events, particularly those in the Olympic games, were known to have had stick and ball games as well. They are believed to have adopted these games from the Egyptians. Ancient Greek artwork is a rare form of proof of these various stick and ball games.

A short while after the Greeks, of course, came the ancient Romans. The Romans developed a sport that had a name. It was called "Paganica" or "Paganicus." The game was played with a bent stick and a leather ball, and players were supposed to hit the ball to various targets, whether it was a tree, a rock, or anything in between. Over time as the Roman Empire expanded, this game spread to countries of Northern Europe and served as a basis for other games that developed.

Many feel that golf is a complicated, highly-skilled game. The truth is it is probably the simplest game known to man, which is why it has been around so long. All you do is take a stick and hit a ball into a hole, nothing hard about that. Anyone from age 2 to 100+ can do it. What makes it difficult is keeping score and trying to do it in the fewest strokes. If you want to have fun and exercise in a beautiful setting with fresh air, just go out and play, and do not worry about your score. More people should do this, and the golf industry should promote it. Ted Williams, the great baseball player, and Sam Snead, the great golfer, were discussing which game was harder: to hit a baseball or to hit a golf ball. Ted argued that hitting a baseball was harder since it was coming towards you at 90 miles an hour while a golf ball just sits there. Sam replied with something along the lines of, "You don't have to play your foul balls, I do."

Golf is so difficult because there are so many variables. At each course, there can be hazards, bunkers, out of bounds, fescue, fast greens, thick rough, tight fairways, etc. You name it, golfers have seen it. Every course is different in its own way. Even a different wind direction on a different day can change how the course plays entirely. It is nearly impossible to get the same exact shot twice on a golf course because there is an endless number of possibilities. No two golf shots are alike, other than maybe a one-inch putt. The lie can be sidehill, downhill, uphill, down in the rough, a flyer lie, basically anything. Then there could be a tree or bunker between the ball and the green, or one can be short sided or have plenty of green to work with. Every situation calls for a different shot, and a golfer needs to know how to hit every single one if he or she wants to succeed at this game. There is no end to the kinds of situations that golfers can find themselves in, so there is no way that they can even practice every kind of shot. Golfers cannot prepare for everything in this game, which may be why they love it. It never gets boring.

GOLF HISTORY ORIGIN

As mentioned previously, golf evolved from various stick and ball games over hundreds of years. The following information is designed to give you a sample of some of those games in chronological order. It is by no means complete, and the dates are approximate. These games are not golf as we know it with a teeing area, fairway, green with hole, played with a set of clubs, a ball, and no defensive opponent.

PRE-HISTORIC - Shepherds: As mentioned earlier, some argue that the first golfers were shepherds over 5,000 years ago. The thought being that they were bored tending their flocks, so they picked up a stick and hit a rock into a gopher hole. Sounds reasonable, but we have no written record. What is interesting about this idea is that they used a hole, which was not used in other stick and ball games. Others were played to targets, such as a tree, or rock, or sticks placed in the ground to create a goal.

5000 BC - POLO

It may seem strange to think of polo as a forerunner of golf because it is played on horseback. However, the players are trained on the ground before they are allowed on the horse, so we have men hitting a ball with a club at a target, much like golf.

1100's - SOULE

Played in France and started very much like the current game of rugby. Players kicked or carried a large ball across a goal. There were defenders, and it was a violent game. However, it evolved into a game with a smaller ball that was hit with a club and no opposition. Sometimes it was played as a race, the winner was the one who got to the goal first, and other times the winner was the player who got to the goal in the fewest strokes, much like golf.

1400's – COLF

This was thought to have been started in The Netherlands and moved to Flanders and Holland. Sometimes played on ice, especially during the Little Ice Age in the 1500's and 1600's. Players used a curved stick to hit a ball to a stake in the ice or a hole during a warmer season. Eventually, they began using wooden clubs with iron heads. The ball was small and made of hard wood, so the game could be played year-round. It was a longer game as far as distance goes because the ball could "go for miles," especially on the ice and with iron club heads. The Flemish making the target a hole in the ground was another step to becoming more like today's golf.

1450 – PALLEMAIL

Pallemail means "ball/mallet." This was a short putting game played with a single club. Eventually, it expanded to several clubs and is the forerunner of croquet, which started around 1850.

1550 – KOLF/KOLVEN

Kolf is an evolution of colf that appeared in the Netherlands as well. Played in all seasons in streets, alleyways, open fields, and even on frozen rivers and canals, it was very similar to colf in almost every way. As it evolved, it became a game that was more about accuracy than distance, so they shortened it up and used a feather-filled leather ball instead of the harder wooden ball. A modern version of it still exists but is played indoors toward a stake in the ground.

1650 – MAIL A LA CHICANE

Another cross-country stick and ball game, several steps closer to golf, mail a la chicane had a pre-determined course rather than just aiming at trees and rocks. Players used lofted clubs to hit to a raised target. It had scoring based on shots, and the winner was the person with the fewest strokes.

1660 – MAIL AU GRAND COUP

This was a mallet game featuring long drives. It was played in an alley with low boards on each side and was up to 1,000 yards long with a width of about 12 feet. A player could drive the ball about 150 yards, and if the ball cleared the boundary to either side, it was "out of bounds." This game had the first reference to a handicap. However, the handicap was not strokes, it was forward tees.

Chapter 2:
GOLF HISTORY TERMS

ALBATROSS – A rare bird, three under par or double eagle.

BIRDIE – One under par. First used in golf around 1900. "Bird" in old English means beautiful. A player hit a great shot, and his partner exclaimed, "That was a bird of a shot." A few holes later, a different player hit a great shot, and one of the players said, "Another "birdie." From there the term spread.

EAGLE – Two under par. Continues with the bird theme.

BOGEY – One over par. Originally a positive term in the late 1800's. A pro was supposed to play a course in even par, and a good amateur would be a bogey golfer. On a few difficult holes, the pro would give the amateur a stroke handicap. They became known as bogey holes. Soon, bogey came to mean one over par on any hole. At first, the difference between par and bogey golf was only a few strokes.

BUNKER – From old Scottish word "bonkar," meaning chest. A bunker is a sand-filled pit which is also considered a hazard (see HAZARD). The term first appeared in 1812 in the Royal and Ancient (R&A) rules of golf.

CADDIE – Derived from the French term "le cadet." Mary, Queen of Scots, played golf in France and used French "cadets" to carry her clubs. The Scots often adopted French terms into their own language, and this was one of those occasions. She brought the practice of using caddies back to Scotland in 1561 and eventually, the Scots began using the term "caddie" in 1634.

CHALLENGE BELT - The original prize given to the winner of the OPEN from 1860 to 1870. It was made of a red Moroccan leather and had a silver buckle that depicted a golfing scene. Each champion of the tournament got to keep the belt until the next OPEN. If a golfer won the tournament for three consecutive years, he became the owner of the belt. This happened in 1870 when Tom Morris Jr. won for his third year in a row and got to keep the belt, leaving no trophy until the Claret Jug was created.

CLARET JUG – The Jug goes to the winner of the OPEN. When Tom Morris Jr. took away the Challenge Belt in 1870, no agreement could be reached by the clubs involved about a new trophy, so there was no tournament in 1871. The winner in 1872, again, was Tom Morris Jr., and he received a medal. The Claret Jug was created in 1873, and the first winner was Tom Kidd. Tom Morris Jr., however, is the first name on the Jug, done retroactively. The official name of the Jug is the Golf Champion Trophy.

CHIP SHOT – A short shot, in the air only a short time, but with a lot of roll.

PITCH SHOT – Longer than a chip, flies in the air more, but with little roll.

DIVOT – Piece of turf in Scottish. Used for fuel and insulation on roofs. When a golfer makes contact with the ball, if they dig up some of the turf, it is called "making a divot."

DORMIE – To sleep. Often used incorrectly, it applies to the team that is ahead in match play when they are up by as many holes as left to play. They are dormie, so they can go to sleep since they cannot lose.

VAULTED DORMIE – To skip over dormie. In match play, if a team is two up with three to play and win the next hole, they go to three up with two to play and are never dormie.

DRIVING RANGE – A place for golfers and non-golfers alike to hit as many golf balls as they want from a designated area to any target (if a target at all). Many assume that the driving range began as a result of golfers' desires to practice without having to pay hefty greens fees to play a golf course. Instead, the idea came from golf instructors that wanted to make money by selling range balls and teaching lessons at the range.

FAIRWAY – A nautical term meaning the smooth water between the hazards. On a golf course, it is the short grass between the thicker rough grass. It is the desired place for your ball to come to rest after a tee shot on a par four or par five.

FLAGSTICK – The first written reference to a flagstick is 1875, but artwork shows they were in use long before that. The only rules about a flagstick is that is must be round, straight, and free of padding. It is recommended that it be at least seven feet tall and skinny enough to let the ball drop in the hole. The most famous flagsticks are not flagsticks at all, but Wicker Baskets used at Merion CC outside Philadelphia. The designer liked many of the aspects of Wicker Baskets, such as the look, the fact that they last longer than flags, and they do not show the wind direction or strength, contributing to a tougher task in guessing what the wind is doing. They have been used at Merion since 1915.

FORE – Means to look out for danger. When a golfer hears "fore" on the course, the danger is generally from behind or to the side. It is short for "before," meaning to look out in front. It originated at St. Andrews, where there were originally 11 holes going out, and the golfer played the same 11 holes back in from the opposite direction. So, when a player heard "fore," it was a warning to look out in front because people were coming in from the other direction.

FOUR BALL – A type of competition format with two-person teams, counting the better ball (score on the hole) of the pair. A format used in the Ryder Cup.

FOURSOMES – Another competition format with two-person teams, but with alternate shot. Another Ryder cup format. "Foursome" is also a casual term that refers to a group that contains four golfers going out to play together.

FRINGE – The apron of fairway-length grass around the green. If using winter rules in your own fairway, the fringe is considered fairway.

GOLF – From the Dutch word "colf" meaning "club" in the 1400's. It does not come from GENTLEMEN ONLY, LADIES FORBIDDEN and is not because all the other four-letter words were taken.

GREEN – Has two meanings, the first being the most modern: the area around the hole where the ball is putted. The second meaning was the original one, as it came from Scottish origin: referring to the entire golf course.

GREENS FEE - How much it costs to play a round of golf at a golf course.

GREENSKEEPER - A person that maintains a golf course, not just the greens.

HANDICAP - Comes from a trading game called "hand in cap" that was popular in the 1600's and 1700's. There were two traders and a referee, and the referee would win if he was good at making things equal or fair for the two players, just as handicaps make the game fairer for golfers. The term "handicap" did not appear until the 1870's, when handicaps involved strokes. The original use of handicaps just moved golfers to a different set of tees for an advantage/disadvantage. Once they switched the system to strokes, there were four or so different stages that the system went through before reaching its modern form.

1. The first version (1700's-1800's) had four options: "third-one" (one stroke every three holes), "half-one" (one stroke every two holes), "one more" (one stroke every hole), and "two more" (two strokes every hole).

2. The second version, implemented in the late 1800's, involved taking a player's average of his or her best three scores of the year at his or her club and subtracting the course's scratch (par) score from it. This method was not popular at first.
   *From here forward, differing versions of handicapping developed in the different regions of the world, but this will focus on what the USGA did.

3. In 1911, after many years of work, the USGA began using a nationwide handicap system using the previous method of averaging the player's best three scores of the year and subtracting the par. The next big development was a par rating (now called USGA Course Rating) for each golf course in 1912. Over time the system went from counting the three best scores in a year, to the top ten ever (1947), to the best 10 of 25 (1958), to what it is now the best 10 of 20 (1967). There was conflict between those dates, but they ended up with a good compromise.

4. The final phase of handicapping involves the development of

the Slope System. A few state golf associations adopted it before the USGA made it a nationwide concept in 1987. Now, a Course and Slope Rating appear on scorecards at every golf course that is registered in the USGA. A member of the USGA can post their scores into the handicap system GHIN, and it will compute a Handicap Index (decimal) that gives a golfer his or her Course Handicap (whole number) at any golf course in the USGA.

HAZARD – From the French in the 1300's, meaning a game of chance. The first hazards were natural on links land, where earth meets the sea. There were also small streams called burns. When golf moved inland, artificial hazards, both sand bunkers and water hazards, were created and deemed to be a "hazard." There are many USGA rules about hazards, most of which involve or result in penalty strokes if players end up hitting their ball into these areas.

HOLE – In the early days, there was no standard hole (size, depth, etc.), and the hole was made in the earth. It got bigger as the day wore on. In 1829, Musselburgh created a hole with a piece of drain pipe that happened to be laying around. This pipe was 4 ¼ inches in diameter and has become the standard today. Nothing scientific about it, just a lucky piece of pipe. The hole must also be at least four inches deep with the hole-liner. If possible, it should begin at least one inch below the putting surface.

HONOR – Seems like a simple concept at first. On the first tee, a random method (flip a coin, flip a tee, throw balls, draw lots, etc.) can be used to decide who plays first. After playing the first hole, the person who had the lowest score on the hole tees off first on the second hole, they have earned the HONOR. Originally, HONOR was called PRIV-

ILEGE. However, there is a difference between friendly play and tournament play, which is also the same as etiquette versus rules. In friendly play, the group can decide on any system they want, ready golf, back tees first if players use different tees, etc. In tournament play, there can be consequences for playing out of turn, but it is quite rare. In match play, hitting a shot out of turn can result in a golfer's competitor making them "cancel" the shot he or she just hit and hit another one from as close to where they just hit from as possible.

MATCH PLAY – Score is kept by holes rather than total strokes. Low score on a hole wins that hole. If both golfers have the same score, the hole is said to be "halved." This was the original form of golf. There is a version called IRISH MATCH PLAY where the winner of the hole gets two points and others get one point. This allows for match play by more than two players.

MEDAL PLAY – Same as stroke play. Total strokes for the round(s) or tournament are counted. Leads to the term MEDALIST, lowest score wins the medal.

MULLIGAN – A do-over shot in golf. Often on the first tee. The origin of the term is in doubt. There are many stories. The one receiving the most credit is that of David Mulligan from Montreal. He was the only one in his group with a car in the 1920's, and the club road was very long and rough. His friends gave him an extra shot on the first tee because his hands were still shaking from driving. Sometimes called a "correction shot" or more specifically, a "breakfast ball" if it is the first shot of the day.

PAR – Comes from a stock exchange term in the late 1800's referring to a stock being below or above par, its normal price. The PAR of a hole is how many strokes it should take a scratch golfer to get the ball in the hole.

PLUS FOURS – A style of pants. The name comes because they are four inches longer than knickers, which are knee length pants. First used in the late 1800's and were popular in the United States in the 1920's.

ROYAL AND ANCIENT GOLF CLUB OF ST. ANDREWS – Formed in 1754 as the Society of St. Andrews Golfers. In 1834, King William IV gave it the present name.

R & A – A separate organization from the Golf Club. It was formed in 2004 and has three main functions: administer the rules of golf (other than United States and Mexico which is under the USGA), organize the OPEN, as well as other competitions, and develop the game of golf.

STABLEFORD – A golf scoring system created by Dr. Frank Stableford of England in 1931 that uses points rather than strokes to determine the winner. There are many systems, but his original scoring method was zero points for two over, one point for a bogey, two points for par, three for birdie, etc. The intent was to speed up play since you could pick up after a double and that a few bad holes would not ruin your day. In the modern world, the Barracuda Championship is a PGA tour event that uses a MODIFIED STABLEFORD scoring system. They took Dr. Stableford's point system and put their own twist on it, offering negative points for over-par scores and positive points for scores under par. The exact points per score go as follows: -3 points for double bogey, -1 for a bogey, 0 for a par, 2 for birdies, 5 for eagles, and 8 for a double eagle.

WINTER RULES – Also known as "preferred lies" or "lift, clean, and place." Used during adverse conditions, such as heavy rain. It is not an official rule of golf, but a local rule by the course. Only the course can declare local rules, not the players, and they are not mandatory. The ball must be marked before lifted, it cannot be moved around by the club head and once replaced, cannot be moved again. Depending on the course and conditions, players may be allowed to place the ball within six inches of where it lies, within a scorecard length, or within a club length, whichever the course decides. Also it can be lift, clean, and place in your own fairway (fairways only) or through the green (anywhere on the course). Once again, the decision is at the discretion of the golf course. Winter rules may hurt your handicap since your score could be lower.

OBSOLETE

AEROSOL – A player who sprays his shots.

BAFF – A former term that has a meaning similar to "fat" or "heavy," describing hitting the ground before the ball.

BUZZARD – A dangerous bird. Two over par or double bogey.

STYMIE – When one ball blocks the path to the hole of the opponent's ball. The original rule in 1744 was unless the balls were touching, neither could be lifted. In 1775, that rule was changed so that if the blocking ball was within six inches, it could be lifted. If more than six inches, the player who was behind had to either play around or over the blocking ball. If that player hit the forward ball, he had to play his play wherever it stopped, and the other player had a choice of replacing or using his new position. If the forward ball was knocked in the hole, it counted as being holed out. At one point, the rule was modified so that the away player could concede the closer putt. In 1952, the stymie rule was abolished because balls could be marked to not interfere with the other golfers' putts.

WATER CLUB – A club that was specially designed to hit shots out of the water. It was not always allowed to take a drop from hazards, so this shot was a more regular occurrence.
* Almost all original golf club names are now obsolete. Examples: mashie, niblick, spoon, brassie.

GOLF SLANG

ACE - a hole-in-one.

ARMY GOLF - When a golfer seems to hit every shot in a different direction. Refers to the "left, right, left" chant used by a marching army.

BEACH - When a ball has found a bunker, that golfer is going to the "beach."

BREAKFAST BALL - A mulligan used on the first tee.

DANCE FLOOR - The putting surface (the green).

DUFFER/HACKER – An incompetent golfer.

DUNK - If a player holes out from off the green by landing it in the hole (no bounces prior), they are said to have "dunked" it.

FAT/DUFF/FLUB/CHILI DIP - If a golfer hits behind the ball, he or she may say they hit the shot "fat," or they "duffed," "flubbed," "chili dipped," or "laid the sod over" it.

FRIED EGG - When a ball plugs (is below the surface of the sand) in a bunker, it leaves an outline in the sand where it splashed in and failed to roll out of it.

FROG HAIR - Another word for the fringe. It comes from the phrase "finer than frog hair." Since frogs do not have hair, it means something very fine. So, in golf, the grass of the fringe is finer than the rough.

HOSEL ROCKET - Also known as a "shank." It is when a player hits a shot so far off the heel of the face (toward the shaft) that it catches the hosel and shoots off to the right.

PILL – Old Dutch, 1400's, meaning a small ball.

SANDBAGGER - Also known as a "Bandit." A player who cheats by inflating his handicap to win bets or tournaments. The term does not come from the sandbag used to prevent floods. In Scotland in the 1800's, crooks would use socks filled with sand to beat people. From there it moved to the world of Poker meaning to deceive your opponents.

SHORT STUFF - The fairway.

TEXAS WEDGE - The name of a shot that is hit with a putter from off the green.

THIN - If a golfer does not touch the ground with his or her club when they make contact with the ball, they have most likely hit it "thin," and the ball will fly lower to the ground.

WORMBURNER/WINDBEATER - An unusually low tee shot that could be the result of a miss-hit (a thin shot) or as the latter term is more benevolent, done on purpose to stay out of the wind.

Chapter 3:
HISTORY OF THE GOLF BALL

1. ROCKS pre-historic
The theory about shepherds being the first to play a prior form of golf says that they were bored, so they picked up a stick and hit a ROCK into a gopher hole. Thus, a ROCK is the first golf ball. This goes back to about 5,000 years ago. Obviously this was not golf as we know it, and there are no written records to support this concept.

2. WOOD 1400-1600
The first man-made golf ball was made of wood. This wooden ball was inherited from older stick and ball games, such as croquet and polo. The age-old question is, "Which came first, the chicken or the egg?" In golf there is no question which came first, "the ball or the club." The ball came first because it was inherited from the older games. Before there was a hole in the ground, golf was really a target game. Cross country golf was played with a rock, tree, or goal as the target.

These balls were made of hardwood, such as Beech. It should be noted that clubs at this time were also made of wood. With wood hitting wood, these balls would only go about 75 yards. They were smooth and had poor flight patterns. Often like a knuckleball, but they were durable. Wooden balls were used on the continent of Europe, but there is no evidence that they reached Scotland.

3. HAIRY 1500's
Basically made of cow hair stuffed in a leather case, then sewn up, and painted. The big advantage over wood is these balls could be driven

150 yards. It also had a better flight pattern than the wooden ball. The problem was that these balls were expensive, not round, and did not last long in wet conditions. As a result, these balls do not have a long life in the history of golf. They were soon replaced by the feathery.

4. FEATHERY 1600-1850

The Feathery was a major improvement over the Hairy. Construction was similar, but the Feathery had two big advantages: it was made with a hat full of wet goose feathers and a case made of wet leather. When they dried, the feathers expanded and the leather shrank, making a very hard ball that could be driven about 200 yards. They were painted white, so they could be more easily found. They were very expensive since an expert ball maker could only make about three balls a day, and they were not durable. Only the wealthy could afford them. A ball cost more than a club.

While a big advancement, the Feathery basically made the wood ball and the Hairy obsolete. However, it still had problems. It was impossible to make perfectly round, it came apart in wet conditions, and lasted for only about two rounds. Losing one was very expensive.

5. GUTTA-PERCHA 1850-1900

Also known as the "guttie" or "gutty." It was made from the dried sap of a Sapodilla tree. When heated, the sap acted like rubber and could be molded. The Gutty killed the feathery because it had four major advantages: it was cheap to make so the masses could afford it, had a better flight pattern (the first ones were smooth, but it was soon discovered that as they became marked up, they performed better. As a result, they were manufactured with grooves shortly after, the beginning of the dimple concept). They lasted a long time, and they were round. Also, they needed less paint, two coats instead of three, which helped their performance. The first ones were painted white for protection and find-ability; for winter play, they were painted red.

In the beginning, the Gutties were made by hand, but soon molds were made so they could be mass produced, which, again, reduced their cost and spread the game of golf.

6. HASKELL 1900

This is the forerunner of the modern golf ball. Invented by Coburn Haskell of the Goodrich Rubber Company, it had a solid rubber core with tight rubber thread wound around the core and a Balata cover. Balata was very soft, and a miss-hit with an iron would make a cut in the cover that looked like a smile and made the ball useless. The Haskell outperformed the Gutty, and the Gutty soon became obsolete. The Haskell added 20 yards to drives. Dimples were added to the Haskell in 1905.

7. MODERN GOLF BALL

In 1967, Spalding made a ball with a tough Syrlin cover that was more durable. Since that time, there has been a proliferation of one, two, and three-piece balls with varying dimple patterns to control spin and feel: the modern ball.

Chapter 4:
HISTORY OF THE GOLF CLUB

The following table gives an APPROXIMATE comparison of antique clubs to the current number system. "Standard" or "matched" sets of clubs did not appear until the 1920's. Prior to that, golfers used to make their own clubs, so all brassies were not the same. The 14-club rule did not take effect until the 1930's; prior to that, it was common for good players or their caddies to carry 20+ clubs. Even in the current era, all clubs are not the same, the 5-iron (30 degrees) from the 1950's is not the same 5-iron [26 degrees] used by today's players. That is part of the reason why today's players hit a 5-iron 200+ yards.

CURRENT	APPROXIMATE ANTIQUE
Driver	Driver, Play Club, Grassed Driver
2 Wood	Brassie
3 Wood	Spoon
5 Wood [or higher]	Baffing Spoon
1 Iron	Driving Iron
2 Iron	Cleek, Mid-Iron
3 Iron	Mid-Mashie
4 Iron	Mashie Iron
5 Iron	Mashie
6 Iron	Spade Mashie
7 Iron	Mashie Niblick
8 Iron	Pitching Niblick
9 Iron	Niblick
Wedge	Jigger, Chipper
Putter	Putter

BRASSIE – Had a brass sole plate

NIBLICK – Means "short nose" in Scottish.

MASHIE – "Sledgehammer" in old Scottish

SABBATH STICKS – The Church of Scotland frowned upon playing golf on Sunday, so clubs were designed to look like walking sticks until the player reached the course.

SPADE MASHIE – A deep face

SPOON – Concave face like a spoon

OTHER COLORFUL GOLF CLUB NAMES OF THE PAST
BENNY – Mallet-headed putter.

CRAN CLEEK – A wood insert in a metal head.

MONGREL MASHIE – Using hickory shafted clubs after steel shafts became standard.

PRESIDENT – Had a hole in the blade to allow hits out of water. Also known as "puddle club" and "water iron." Named "President" because the hole in the center made it "clear headed."

RAKE IRON – Blade looked like a rake. Used from the sand or tall grass.

RUTTING IRON – A small headed iron to pick the ball out of tree roots.

URQUHART ADJUSTABLE – An iron with an adjustable head for different lofts all the way down to putter. It claimed to be "ten clubs in one." The product created a family business run by, you guessed it, the Urquharts.

* Some of the following names may not agree with the names above. That is because names changed over time.

WOOD 1400–1900

In the early days, people made their own clubs. As the game grew and became more affordable, professionals made clubs. The shafts were generally made from Ash and the heads from hardwoods, such as Beech. There were no standards. Drivers had long, thin heads. The clubs were not numbered as they are today, but had names. In 1502, King James IV of Scotland had a set of clubs made by a bow-maker. The set consisted of the following:

- LONGNOSE – Driver
- GRASSED DRIVER – Fairway wood
- SPOON – Iron
- NIBLICK – Wedge
- CLEEK – Putter

Around 1850, Hickory, imported from the United States, was used to make shafts. Hickory is stronger and more durable than Ash. It is interesting to note that the development of the club follows the development of the ball. As the ball was improved from wood, to Hairy, to Feathery, to Gutta-Percha, to Haskell, the club was changed to take advantage of the characteristics of the new ball. The changes in clubs are more gradual and less dramatic than the changes in balls.

METAL 1900

While there were some metal heads prior to this time, they were made for special shots, such as out of ruts, etc. A miss-hit with a metal club also caused more damage to a Feathery than a wooden club. They were heavy and poorly made, so they did not catch on until forged metal was used.

SCHENECTADY PUTTER

The first center shafted, smooth faced putter. Invented by Arthur Knight of the Mohawk Golf Club in Schenectady, New York. Used by Walter Travis to win the 1903 United States Amateur and the 1904 British Amateur (first foreigner to win it). The Royal and Ancient Golf Club banned the putter in 1910, deeming it gave players an "unfair advantage." Once they realized that perhaps it was the player's skills, not the putter that gave them an advantage, they repealed the ban on center-shafted putters in 1951.

GROOVES 1908

The first forged metal blades had a smooth surface. Grooves were introduced in 1908 because golfers found they could get more control and better spin with grooves.

WHISTLER 1915

A type of steel shaft that never caught on, but it was the first playable one. Patented by Allan Lard, it was a solid steel shaft that had many tiny holes in it to make it lighter. When swung, the small holes made a whistling noise due to the wind entering and exiting them, hence the name. An important step toward a mainstreamed steel shaft.

PERSIMMON WOODS 1920

Introduced during the 1920's, Persimmon was a very hard wood that produced more distance on drives. There was an insert in the face that was screwed in place and led to the expression, "I hit it on the screws," meaning the sweet spot. The expression is still used today, even though metal heads do not have screws on the face. The clubfaces were smaller than modern woods, especially modern drivers, so a miss-hit was much less forgiving. Once technology made advancements, a few tour players held onto their persimmons for a little while, but most made the switch to metal drivers very quickly.

STEEL SHAFTS 1924

Steel shafts were introduced far earlier than 1924, but they were legalized by the USGA in 1924 and by the Royal & Ancient in 1929 but did not become dominant over wooden shafts until the 1930's. Blacksmiths experimented with steel shafts in the 1890's, but due to a lack of technologies we have today, they were solid steel, and therefore very heavy and impractical. In 1910, Arthur F. Knight, inventor of the Schenectady Putter, had made a patented steel shaft, but could not get enough support to get it legalized by the USGA and R&A. There were a few other attempts to create a practical and legal steel shaft, such as the WHISTLER (above), but the first one to be successful in making a shaft very similar to the one that is used today was a company in the U.S. called Bristol Steel. It was a seamless, tubular shaft and served as a basis for every advancement in steel shafts following it. They were far superior to Hickory because they were more durable and more consistent in performance. By the 1930's, steel shafts became the standard thanks to True Temper's development of the tapered shaft in 1929.

SAND WEDGE 1930

Gene Sarazen did not invent the sand wedge. Scots had been using special clubs to hit out of sand bunkers for many years before. What he did do was design the modern sand wedge with a steel shaft, plenty of loft, and a large flange (sole) that allows the club to slide through the sand. Today, we refer to this as "bounce" or "degrees of bounce."

CAST IRONS 1960

There are two ways to make irons: they are forged or cast. Forged means that they begin as a hunk of metal and are shaped by tools until they are in the proper form. Cast irons are where molten metal is poured into a mold until it hardens, coming out in the perfect shape. It is much cheaper to make cast irons, therefore this invention helped grow the game of golf by making it more affordable for the masses.

GRAPHITE SHAFTS 1968

Introduced by Frank Thomas to be tested in 1968, these shafts are lighter in weight than say, steel shafts, and therefore allows the golfer to generate more clubhead speed. The ultimate result is extra distance, which is why today, they are in all clubs that are meant to go farther, such as drivers, woods, and hybrids. Irons with graphite shafts are also catching on. Though technology has lightened steel shafts over the years, they can only be made so light, which is why these graphite shafts are even more important for older or younger golfers that have slower swing speeds. At first, graphite was very expensive, but as time went on, they have become less and less expensive; good news for the golfing masses.

METAL WOODS 1970

The origin of the metal wood is interesting. Owners of driving ranges in the United States asked manufacturers to make metal woods because the wooden ones were not durable. Manufacturers were reluctant because of the sound the metal woods made, they felt golfers would be turned off by that. Clearly that did not stop them from catching on.

GINTY 1973

The "Ginty" was a club designed specifically for the average golfer to get out of trouble, such as deep rough. It was invented by Stan Thompson, a clubmaker who started his own golf business. His first Ginty was a 7-wood head on a 4-wood shaft. The head gave the golfer more loft, which can be easier to hit well, while the longer shaft created more clubhead speed. Although the clubhead was made of wood, there was also a sole plate inserted into the clubhead that was made of zinc. The plate gave the club a lower center of gravity, contributing more to the loft of the club and allowing the golfer to hit the ball even higher. It is supposed to be able to get a ball out of virtually any lie.

BAFFLER 1975

Introduced by Cobra, this club was the first utility wood. Similar to the Ginty, the Baffler utilized a sole plate to create a lower center of gravity, making it easy for golfers to get out of poor lies. The plate created two runners on the bottom of the head, cutting through grass with ease. At the time, the Ginty and the Baffler were competitors in this new category of golf clubs. Eventually, they resulted in what are now known as hybrids.

HYBRIDS late 1900's-early 2000's

A combination of a wood and an iron that makes hitting a club with long-iron loft much easier. Although it is a relatively recent development, the roots of hybrids go way back to the days of wooden clubs. Back then, their woods were basically hybrids because the shape was similar, if not the same. Hybrids have a thinner head, whereas a modern wood has a head that goes further back, so it is wider. Woods back then had a much slimmer head than modern woods, so the inspiration for the head shape of a hybrid must have come from the past.

Chapter 5:
HISTORY OF MAJORS

PGA

At the present, there are four tournaments that are considered majors – The Masters, U.S. Open, the Open (British), and the PGA Championship. However, the history of Majors is relatively recent considering the long history of golf. The Master's only started in 1934. If one player wins all four, it is considered the "Grand Slam" of golf. While five golfers have completed the modern Grand Slam, there is one golfer that has completed the Grand Slam in a single year before the Masters came about, so it consisted of the British Amateur and Open Championships, as well as the United States Amateur and Open Championships. This person was Bobby Jones in 1930. Since the two amateur championships were in this Grand Slam, only an amateur could complete it at the time, which is partially why The Masters came about. This tournament would offer professionals a chance to complete their own Grand Slam. A few professionals have come close to winning all four majors in one year, such as Tiger Woods, who won four in a row from 2000 to 2001, but none have won all four in a single year.

MASTERS – The only major played on the same course every year: Augusta National Golf Club. Started in 1934, Bobby Jones was a co-founder along with Cliff Roberts. It is an Invitational Tournament with the smallest and probably the weakest field of all the majors. The winner receives the famous Green Jacket. Jack Nicklaus has won the most green jackets at Augusta, winning a total of six times.

U.S. OPEN – Started in 1895 and run by the United States Golf Association, it is generally considered the most difficult of the majors because of course set up. Players can qualify to enter. Women are not excluded, but none have qualified. The U.S. Open began as a one-day, 36-hole competition with a playing field consisting of ten professionals and one amateur. Oakmont Country Club has hosted this tournament a total of nine times, including the recent 2016 U.S. Open, which is more than any other course. The most wins of the U.S. Open by one person is four, but four people have done it: Willie Anderson, Bobby Jones, Ben Hogan, and Jack Nicklaus.

THE OPEN (British) – The oldest of the majors, beginning in 1860. The idea for this tournament came from two men, Earl of Eglinton and Colonel James Fairlie, in response to the death of golfer Allan Robertson. Robertson was no doubt the best golfer at the time, so a new Champion golfer needed to be crowned. The tournament used to be run by the three original golf clubs that it rotated around in the beginning: Royal and Ancient Golf Club at St. Andrews, Prestwick, and The Honourable Company of Edinburgh Golfers, who started at Musselburgh Links until they moved to Muirfield in 1891. Ever since 1920, the Royal and Ancient (R&A) has had full responsibility of running the tournament. The tournament is generally held on links style courses in Scotland and England, although one of the fourteen past venues exists in Northern Ireland (Royal Portrush). Generally, the course is not set up harder than normal, and the course's defense is the weather. Players can qualify to enter. St. Andrews has hosted the OPEN 29 times, much more than any other club. Harry Vardon has the most wins of the Open, having won the tournament six times. The winner receives the Claret Jug, the most famous trophy in all of golf, however, for the first ten years, the winner received the "Challenge Belt."

PGA CHAMPIONSHIP – Run by the PGA OF AMERICA, which is different than the PGA Tour, this tournament started in 1916. The PGA OF AMERICA is the organization made up mainly of club professionals, and the tournament reserves spots for these individuals. It is nicknamed "glory's last chance" since it is the last of majors to be played each year. However, there are plans to move this tournament to May in 2019, so it may lose this nickname. From 1916 to 1957, it was match play. It switched to medal play in 1958. Southern Hills CC has hosted it the most, which is four times. Walter Hagen and Jack Nicklaus have each won it five times, but Hagen's victories occurred when the tournament was still match play.

LPGA

The LPGA currently has five majors, but in the past, it has had as few as two. All the worldwide governing bodies of men's golf agree on the four majors, but that is not the case with women's golf. As a result, the number and titles of the women's majors have not been as stable or consistent over the years. The LPGA did not exist prior to 1950, but they retroactively list winners of various events all the way back to 1930, which has caused a bit more confusion.

The current five in order of which they are played each year are:

ANA INSPIRATION – ANA stands for All Nippon Airways, the Japanese airline that sponsors the tournament. However, the LPGA organizes the event. The prior name was the Kraft Nabisco Championship and before that, the Dinah Shore. It goes back to 1983 as a major. It is the LPGA equivalent of the Master's in that it is played on the same course each year, and they give a White Robe instead of a Green Jacket. It has also become famous for the winner jumping into "Poppie's Pond" at the end of the tournament. Amy Alcott, Betsy King, and Annika Sorenstam have all won that right the most times, three.

WOMEN'S PGA CHAMPIONSHIP – This tournament is the second-oldest major in women's golf (behind the Women's U.S. Open), dating back to 1955. In the past, it was organized by the LPGA, but as of 2015, it has been organized by the PGA of America. When it was still run by the LPGA, the event would settle at one course for a few years and then move, instead of changing location every year, which is what it does now. The current sponsor is KPMG since they began sponsoring it in 2015, but there have been many previous sponsors, such as Wegman's (2010-2014) and McDonald's (1994-2009). Only one woman has won this tournament four times, Mickey Wright.

U.S. WOMEN'S OPEN – The oldest major in women's golf, originating in 1946. Currently organized by the USGA, but in the beginning, the short-lived Women's Professional Golfers Association (WPGA) ran it for the first three years until the LPGA began forming. The LPGA organized it from 1949 to 1952, when they handed it over to the USGA. Courses rotate, but Atlantic City CC and Pine Needles L & GC have both hosted it three times, more than any other club.

WOMEN'S BRITISH OPEN – The Ladies' Golf Union of Ireland and the United Kingdom is responsible for running this tournament. It has existed since 1976, but only became a major in 2001, replacing the du Maurier Classic as the (at the time) fourth major. Courses rotate. Woburn has hosted this event the most, totaling ten times in just 41 years of existence. Often referred to as the "RICOH Women's British Open" since Ricoh became the sponsor in 2007.

EVIAN CHAMPIONSHIP – The tournament has been around since 1994, but has only been classified as a major since 2013. When it was a regular women's event, it was called the Evian Masters. Evian is a corporation noted for its natural spring water. The tournament is organized by the Ladies European Tour (LET). It is always played at the same course at the Evian Resort in France. The only major, either for men or women, that is not played in the United States or Great Britain.

There are three other tournaments that have been considered majors in the past.

The Women's Western Open (1930–1967) – This event was organized by the Women's Western Golf Association. It was match play from 1930-1954 until it became 72-hole stroke play in 1955, which lasted until its final year in 1967. The tournament was discontinued for unknown reasons.

Titleholders Championship (different dates from 1937–1972) – This tournament took place at Augusta CC. Due to its location, it was kind of the women's version of The Masters during its existence. It also began the tradition of giving the champion a green jacket before The Masters began doing so in 1949. The final year that Augusta CC hosted this event was 1966, but it was held again in 1972 in North Carolina.

Du Maurier Classic (1979-2000) – This tournament has been held since 1973 and still exists, but it was only considered a major during the dates above and has changed names multiple times. When it began in 1973, it was called "La Canadienne" because it was and still is played in Canada, until it became the Peter Jackson Classic the following year and held that title until 1979. Up until 1979, it was just a regular tournament, but once it gained the title du Maurier Classic, it became a major. In 2001, it was replaced by the Women's British Open. Since then, the now regular tournament has changed sponsors multiple times, but is currently called the Canadian Pacific Women's Open.

Chapter 6:
TOUR PLAYOFFS - FEDEX CUP
AND CME GROUP

FEDEX CUP

A recent development in the history of golf is the FEDEX CUP for PGA TOUR players. The concept was developed in 2005 and first awarded in 2007. Basically it is a season-long event followed by a four-tournament playoff. Tour players accumulate points in regular season tournaments. Generally, 500 points are awarded for winning an event and smaller amounts for the lower finishers. At the end of the season, the top 125 players are eligible for the playoffs. The points are increased for the playoff tournaments, 2000 points for winning and so on down the line.

After the first playoff event, the top 100 advance to the second round. After that, the best 70 go on to the third round, and the top 30 make the final tournament called the TOUR CHAMPIONSHIP. Over the years, there have been some rule changes. In 2008, they implemented a "reset" of point distributions when players reached the playoffs and awarding more points to playoff event winners compared to the win of a regular season event. This was an immediate result of Vijay Singh's accumulation of enough points during the season and the first few playoff events to win the cup without having to play the final tournament. In other words, it was designed to penalize a player for skipping a playoff event. The winners of the FEDEX CUP by year are as follows:

2007 - Tiger Woods

2008 - Vijay Singh

2009 - Tiger Woods

2010 - Jim Furyk

2011 - Bill Haas

2012 - Brandt Snedeker

2013 - Henrik Stenson

2014 - Billy Horschel

2015 - Jordan Spieth

2016 - Rory McIlroy

2017 - Justin Thomas

Out of the 11 winners, eight are Americans, while the other three countries are Fiji, Sweden, and Northern Ireland. The winner of the cup gets $10 million out of the $35 million purse, second get $3 million, third, $2 million, fourth, $1.5 million, and fifth, $1 million, down to $32,000 for last place. Originally the $10 million was a tax deferred retirement annuity that now is a combination of an annuity and cash. When calculating top money winners, this $10 million bonus is not included.

Since 2013, the top 125 players in the FEDEX points standings get their Tour card for the following year, and the winner gets a five-year exemption for the PGA Tour. Players 126-150 on the FEDEX points list are awarded conditional PGA status, in which they can play on the Web.com to better their chances of retaining their Tour card. Previously, the money list determined both.

Once it gets down to the final event, the Tour Championship, any of the 30 players have a chance to win the FEDEX CUP, but the odds of someone winning outside the top five are relatively low. If any of the top five players win, they are guaranteed to win the entire Fedex Cup. Someone in the top five can win the whole thing, even if they do not win the Tour Championship, as happened in 2017. Xander Schauffele won the Tour Championship, but Justin Thomas won the FEDEX CUP with a second-place finish.

The top ten FEDEX CUP money winners rounded to the nearest million are:

1. Tiger Woods $25
2. Rory Mcllroy $16
3. Jim Furyk $15
4. Jordan Spieth $15
5. Henrik Stenson $14
6. Brandt Snedeker $12
7. Bill Haas $11
8. Vijay Singh $11
9. Billy Horschel $11
10. Justin Thomas $10

These players have won the $10 million prize, but Tiger is the only one to do it twice. Two interesting names are not on this list – Dustin Johnson is 11th with $9 million and Phil Mickelson is 13th with $8 million. Steve Stricker squeezes in 12th place with $9 million.

CME Group

As for the LPGA, they, too, have developed their own version of a season-ending championship. In its first true appearance as a season-ending "playoff," it was called the LPGA Playoffs at the ADT and took place 2006-2008 (preceded the FEDEX CUP). Previously, the ADT Championship was just another LPGA event on the tournament schedule. Qualifying for this event was limited to 32 players. To qualify, the season was split into halves, in which the top 15 point winners from each half made it to the Championship. Winners of LPGA majors and a few other events were automatically included in this top 15. After the first half, points were cleared so that the second half started with an even playing field. The remaining two exemptions were extended to two "wildcards," one from each half, typically the top money winners who did not already qualify. The first-place finisher won a $1 million prize. ADT did not extend its sponsorship, so the event was replaced by the LPGA Tour Championship in 2009.

In contrast to the ADT Championship, the LPGA Tour Championship playing field consisted of the top 120 money winners for the year. The top prize for this season-ending event was $225,000. This event had an even shorter life than its predecessor, lasting only 2009 and 2010 until it was replaced by the CME Group Titleholders. Each season-ending event that has been mentioned is considered separate from the others.

The CME Group Titleholders held its title during the years 2011-2013, and players qualified by placing in the top three in any LPGA Tour event that occurred throughout the year. If a player finished top three in another tournament following their first top three, qualifying would extend to the fourth-place finisher, and so on. The name of the tournament and qualifying methods were changed in 2014.

What the LPGA has now is the "Race to the CME Globe." Similar to the FEDEX CUP, this is a season-long points system that has top-finishers of other Tour events winning a certain amount of points that accumulate. Only LPGA Tour members are allowed to win points, and the top 72 players at the end of the season qualify for the tour championship, renamed in 2014 as the CME Group Tour Championship. After the 72 players qualify, the points are reset based on players' positions after the points race. The way this redistribution happens, the top three players going into the Tour Championship are guaranteed to win the title with a win at the Championship, and the top-9 have the chance to win the title, depending on how the players ahead of them in points finish. The first-place finisher wins a $500,000 prize, except in 2013 when it was $700,000.

The winners of the ADT Championship:
    2006: Julieta Granada
    2007: Lorena Ochoa
    2008: Ji-Yai Shin

The winners of the LPGA Tour Championship:
    2009: Anna Nordqvist
    2010: Maria Hjorth

The winners of each CME Group Championship:
    2011: Hee Young Park
    2012: Na Yeon Choi
    2013: Shanshan Fang
    2014: Lydia Ko
    2015: Christie Kerr
    2016: Charley Hull
    2017: Ariya Jutanugarn

Chapter 7:
HISTORY OF WOMEN'S GOLF

Background:

The earliest involvement of women in the game of golf is thought by some to be through the featherie golf ball. In ancient Greece, royalty and royal princesses played a hand-ball game that used a leather ball filled with feathers, just like one of the earliest golf balls. The story of this ancient game begins with a story of a woman named Anagalla, inventing the ball, and teaching Princess Nausica how to play handball. This story comes from the *Rules of Thistle Golf Club*.

One of the more well-known tales of women in golf is that of Mary, Queen of Scots. Mary Stuart was a very athletic woman, and she participated in most of the usual sports for women at that time (mid 1500s), such as tennis and archery. However, she also hunted, which has always been considered by many to be a job for men. Her enemies also accused her of playing maile (pall mall) and golf, because how dare a woman play male sports? Although it is unclear whether she was golfing, putting, or just playing maile, there was a sighting of Mary playing tennis wearing men's garb, so there is no doubt that she would be audacious enough to play golf. Thus Mary, Queen of Scots, was very likely the first woman to play golf.

In Musselburgh, Scotland, as early as the late 1700's, women were known to play golf on their days off from work. These ladies were known as "fishwives." In Musselburgh, women were expected to "do the work of men," and they played sports like the men as well. In 1811, the golf club that would become Royal Musselburgh Golf Club decided to officially support the women by hosting a competition for them with actual prizes. This may be the first match involving women with prizes involved, but it was definitely not the first ever golf match between two women. In 1738, two women played golf against each other at Brunts-field Links in Scotland, with their husbands as caddies. The one Edin-burgh paper that covered the match said the winner was "charming Sally." She is the first ever named golfer to play in a match.

A recent discovery found a first ever female club maker/repairer. David Denholm was a club-maker at Bruntsfield Links, the venue that held the first ladies golf match (above). When he died, his wife, Isobel Denholm took over the business and became the first female club-maker. This information was found in an Edinburgh Business Directory where she was listed as a club-maker from 1820 to 1823. It appears that Brunts-field Links was an important place for the beginnings of women's golf.

One of the biggest obstacles to women who wanted to play golf was finding a venue that would allow them to do so. In the mid-1800's, a woman by the name of Mrs. Wolfe-Murray played regularly at St. An-drews. However, she received much comment and criticism from the public. In 1867, St. Andrews also served as the location for the first ever women's golf club. First Named the "St. Andrews Ladies Golf Club," it was renamed twice by switching out "Golf Club" for "Putting Club." By 1886, this club had 500 members. It was, and still is, just that, a Put-ting Club. "The Himalayas" is an 18-hole putting green near the Club-house for visitors, so it can be accessed by the public. It is still open today, and tourists can play the course for just a £3 greens fee for adults or £1 for seniors and children.

Back in the mid-1800's, there were also golf courses meant specif-ically for women. The oldest women's golf course was at North Berwick, Scotland. It was built in 1867 and once the ladies club formed there in 1887, they were responsible for paying for the lease, as well as hiring workers to maintain the course until 1935. They even had their own clubhouse. This course obviously was not the first course to have ladies play on it, but it was the first ever "ladies course."

Ladies Golfing Union:

The first ever women's golf association began in the United Kingdom. It was called the Ladies Golf Union (LGU), and it was formed in 1893. Since most golf clubs were only available to male golfers at the time, this Union became an opportunity for golf clubs to become inclusive to women as well. A few years before the Union was founded, there were only about ten ladies clubs in existence in the UK. Many golf historians believe that the number was higher since the list was missing a few obvious ones. By 1892, a year before the Union started, there were already at least 49 known ladies clubs in Great Britain alone. Once the Union was formed, clubs joined in at a moderate rate. The growth must have been exponential because while there were only 41 clubs in it in 1899, there were 400 by 1914.

The foundation of the Ladies Golfing Union in the United Kingdom must have been inspiration to golfing ladies in other countries because they formed Unions as well. The Irish Ladies Golfing Union began shortly after the LGU the same year, 1893. This was only two years after the men's version of the Union formed. Then in 1904, the Welsh Ladies Golfing Union and the Scottish Ladies Golfing Association formed. It is quite notable that these two organizations were formed before their men's counterparts.

The LGU is also accredited with developing a sensible handicap system. They implemented the system in 1896, and the main leader in this development was Miss Issette Pearson. She took the authority to assign "handicap advisers" to the clubs in the Union and have them assign each course a women's course rating instead of relying on the club to do it. Having the same people go club to club made sure that there was no bias and that the ratings were consistently fair. It took some time to develop, but the LGU did what the men had failed to do before them, create a handicap system that was efficient at making golf an even playing field from course to course.

Along with the LGU, the first British Ladies Championship came about. Held in the same year as the foundation of the LGU, 1893, the tournament had 38 ladies competing in it. Lytham & St. Annes was the first course to host it, but now rotates amongst many courses in Scotland. The first champion was Lady Margaret Scott, who dominated the game until she retired in 1897. Since this was initially a British tournament set up by the British golfing union for women, no Scottish ladies competed in it until 1897. However, that year, the Championship hosted an astounding 102 golfers, British and Scottish. The United States hosted their own championship for women beginning in 1895, but the level of golf was far more advanced in Europe.

Women Golf Course Architects:

When thinking of golf's greatest architects, there are many names that come to mind, such as Robert Trent Jones, Donald Ross, Tom Fazio, and Pete Dye, all men. When it comes to golf history, there is not much talk about women golf course architects. However, though there are many fewer female architects in the game, they have played an important role in streamlining golf for women. The first female golf course architect in the United States (if not the world) was Ida Dixon. She designed Springhaven Club in Pennsylvania in 1904, where they now hold a tournament every year in honor of her.

Most women architects that came after Ida Dixon were great golfers that turned to golf course architecture once they passed their prime. Perhaps the most well-known or notable of these women is Alice Dye. Yes, she is Pete Dye's wife, but she is known for much more than just that. She was one of the best amateurs in the country during the 1950's and 1960's, winning more than 50 amateur events during her career. One of Alice's biggest accomplishments as far as architecture goes is her "Two Tee System" diagram that she published in the 1970's. Back then there were no reasonable-distance courses for women that had high handicaps. This made the game possibly less enjoyable for women because it took them so many strokes just to get to the green. Alice's idea was to have two tee options for women, so that they could play the proper distance for their individual games. Clearly her proposal caught on. Now you can see at least three or four sets of tees at every golf course.

Alice has done great work on her own, but being Pete Dye's wife also offered some great input in the design of several of his most famous golf courses. Pete and Alice were a sort of "dream team" from the very start. Some of her more well-known work can be seen on courses like Harbour Town Golf Links, Whistling Straits, and Kiawah's Ocean Course. Her most prominent architectural idea was that of the Island Green, the 17th hole at TPC Sawgrass. All her accomplishments, including becoming the president of the American Society of Golf Course Architects (ASGCA), resulted in Alice Dye receiving the 2017 ASGCA Donald Ross Award. This award signifies the impact she had on the game of golf, as well as the golf course architect profession.

Today, we see LPGA players that want to stay involved in the game, turn to architecture once they retired from playing professionally. This trend is thought to be started by Jan Stephenson, an Australian professional who won 16 LPGA events, three of them being majors, as well as many other international tournaments. She actually interned with the Dye's before going out on her own and designing Walkabout Golf Club in Florida. Other LPGA professionals have followed in Stephenson's footstep. Nancy Lopez and Annika Sorenstam have begun designing their own golf courses. Annika's can be found all over the world. In fact, her seven courses are in six different countries.

Fashion:

Golf fashion is something that has changed dramatically over the years and seems to continue to change rapidly even today. In the 1800 and

1900's, men typically wore clothes of the day, consisting of brightly colored jackets to make sure players in other groups could see them in case of a wayward shot. Women, since it was the Victorian era, wore multiple layers of thick clothing. That was their everyday garb, and so it was what they wore to play golf. Of course, this was very constricting, making it nearly impossible to even swing a golf club. This is likely the reason that the first women's golf club was a Putting Club at St. Andrews. A putting stroke would have been much easier to make than a full swing.

The next era, Edwardian, called for a style of dress that was not much more helpful to female golfers. We still see multiple layers involved that made a swing very difficult. Miss Issette Pearson, founder of the LGU, as well as developer of the first realistic handicap system, was a golfer herself, somehow doing it all while dressed like this. Modesty was very important back then, sometimes the long garments got in the way, even making it impossible to see the golf ball when taking a stance. For this reason, women often wore bands to keep their clothing in place. Younger women at the time wore much simpler outfits with only one thin layer (such as a blouse) rather than several thick layers.

It was not until the early 1900's that women golfers showing ankles became acceptable. Before 1933, women always wore skirts. The only thing that changed was the length of it. In the 1920's, the flapper era for women, golf attire was still the same as street clothes, but the skirts were shorter, and the thickness of the clothes was much more practical. The shoes women wore were interesting because there were no golf shoes for women back then, or at least it was unpopular to wear them, so they just wore their everyday shoes. These consisted of flats or clog-style shoes that seem very impractical now. In 1933, Gloria Minoprio, an interesting individual who played with only one golf club, she was the first woman to wear pants, later termed "slacks," on a golf course. She also wore practical golf shoes, typically flats or clog-style shoes. Her outfit was so notable that it can be found in the

British Golf Museum at St. Andrews. Women also started to wear the same style of hat that men typically wore.

For men, the 1940's is when golf fashion began the trend toward modern-day golf wear. Instead of expensive, formal attire, it became more relaxed, allowing shorts and trousers instead of knickers, short-sleeved shirts instead of ties and suits. From there, the only things that changed were fabrics and how the clothes fit. In the 1990's and early-mid 2000's, sleeves on shirts were very wide, and pants were generous. Nowadays, golf clothes offer more of an "athletic fit" that keeps the swing free and fits correctly.

Some articles of clothing, such as the "jogger" style pant that cinches at the ankle, have brought about some controversy over whether some things should be prohibited from golf courses or just the PGA Tour. Nike has developed what they are calling the "blade collar," which is not really a collar at all, so it once again calls on what kind of dress code changes have to or should be made.

As for women, things have changed even more dramatically, calling for actual changes in the LPGA dress guidelines. From the 1920's-1970's, women's golf attire saw a gradual shortening of skirts and more practical short-sleeved polos. The 1970's were when the most modernizing shifts happened. Golf shoes were more practical, and shirts were becoming more modern. Form-fitting pants and shorts were introduced, as well as shorter skirts (but only slightly above the knee). Some Tour players even wore collarless shirts, which is still controversial today. Once the 1990's came around, sleeves started disappearing on women's shirts. Now, there are sleeveless shirts without collars, and skirts that are deemed "too short." The LPGA took action in 2017 to ban skirts that reveal a golfer's "bottom area" and the racerback sleeveless golf shirt without a collar. It can be a racerback, it just must have a collar. With still a lot of controversy, regulations could change quickly.

Chapter 8:
THE GOLF CHANNEL

"WHO'D OF THUNK IT"

A television station that devoted 24 hours a day to a single sport. Unheard of, and it made no sense at the time of its origin. Yet, it happened and became very successful.

The idea was the brainchild of Joseph Gibbs of Birmingham, Alabama. During the 1990 PGA Championship at Shoal Creek Country Club in Birmingham, he hosted Arnold Palmer in his guest house. That was the beginning of a friendship. In 1991, Mr. Gibbs, who was in the media business, had the idea for THE GOLF CHANNEL. He hired the GALLUP POLL to find out if there was enough public interest in the idea. The results were positive, but he needed a big-name golfer to make it succeed. There was none bigger than Arnold Palmer. Thus, Mr. Gibbs contacted Arnold, who was reluctant at first, since Mr. Gibbs wanted Mr. Palmer to put up some of his own money. Arnold finally saw the light, and the two of them raised $80 million and launched THE GOLF CHANNEL in January of 1995. Many of their investors were major cable operators, so they had a built-in distribution system. Mr. Palmer became Chairman, and Mr. Gibbs, Vice Chairman in charge of day-to-day operations.

Five years later, Comcast bought 55% of THE GOLF CHANNEL for $369 million. As we say on the Pro Tour, Mr. Palmer and Mr. Gibbs made a killing.

THE GOLF CHANNEL started as a premier cable station with a limited viewership. Their first broadcast of a golf tournament was the Dubai Desert Classic in January of 1995. In September 1995, they switched to regular cable and thus available to the masses. Viewership exploded, and now over 100 million watch the channel. In addition to the United States, the channel is available in Canada, South America, and Asia.

In 1996, they created a website which allows golf fans the ability to keep up with the all the news in the golf world. In 2007, they became an official channel to broadcast tournaments. In addition to tournaments, the channel shows scores from around the world, provides lessons from pros, has talk shows and special events like the BIG BREAK, which serves as an opportunity for newly-turned professionals to win money and gain exemptions into Tour events, and the HANEY PROJECT, which tries to improve the golf game of celebrities. They also broadcast events for the Champions, LPGA, and European tours. In 2008, they won an EMMY for advancements in technology. In 2011, they broadcasted over 300 hours of men's and women's golf from the Olympics. In 2016, they merged with NBC sports.

In 2008 THE GOLF CHANNEL changed its official name to GOLF CHANNEL for branding purposes. Headquarters are in Orlando, Florida.

As a side note, there was a GOLF CHANNEL UK from 2003 to 2007, but it folded due to a lack of advertisers. There is also a GOLF CHANNEL LATIN AMERICA which broadcasts in Spanish.

Chapter 9:
Golf by Century

GOLF HISTORY 1400's

1457 – Golf banned by James II of Scotland because it interferes with archery training of his military.

1471 – Golf ban reaffirmed by James III.

1480 – In a prayer book dated around this year, a Flemish golfer was depicted on his knees putting to a hole in the ice canal they were playing colf on. Some argue that they were first to use a hole as the target for a stick and ball game. This image illustrated how putting was an important part of their game, which makes it even more closely related to modern golf.

1491 – James IV reaffirms the ban on golf, but orders a set of clubs for himself.

GOLF HISTORY 1500's

1502– Treaty of Glasgow between England and Scotland is signed. Golf had been banned by a series of Scottish kings. That ban is now lifted.

1522– First commoner to play golf. Up until then, only Royals played golf.

1552– First recorded golf at St. Andrews. There probably was golf played before this, but there is not written record.

1567– Mary, Queen of Scots, plays golf. The first known female golfer. She is criticized for playing right after her husband dies.

1592– The Royal Burgh of Edinburgh bans golf on Sunday because it interferes with church.

1618– Invention of the Feathery golf ball. This was a ball made with wet feathers stuffed into wet leather. As the feathers dried, they expanded and as the leather dried, it contracted, making for a very hard ball.

1621- First reference to golf on the links at Dornoch in Northern Scotland.

1642- Aberdeen gained a licensed ball-maker, a man named John Dickson.

1659– Many refer to this year as the first mention of golf in the United States. A law was passed in Fort Orange, now Albany, New York, that stated:

"The Honorable Commissary and Magistrates of Fort Orange and the village of Beverwyck, having heard of divers complaints from the burghers of this place against the practice of playing golf along the streets, which causes great damage to the windows of the houses and also exposes people to the danger of being injured and is contrary to the freedom of the public streets;

Therefore, their honours, wishing to prevent the same, hereby forbid all persons to play golf in the street, under the penalty of forfeiture of Fl. 25 for each person who shall be found doing so. Thus, done in Fort Orange, at the meeting of the honorable court of the said place on the tenth day of December, Anno 1659."

This is a poor English translation from the Dutch language. It clearly is not golf as we know it since golf is not played on streets. It was probably the Dutch game called Kolven, which is more like field hockey.

1672– Oldest recorded golf match that was documented. Sir John Foulis, a lawyer in Edinburgh, kept very detailed records of his rounds and played at Musselburgh with his friends Gosford, Lyon, and others. Apparently, he lost to them.

1687– Oldest golf instruction journal, written by Thomas Kincaid. It also contained instructions on how to make clubs. It was not considered the first ever golf instruction book because it was never published, it was just a handwritten journal for personal use.

GOLF HISTORY 1700's

1744– First golf club in the world. Honourable Company of Edinburgh Golfers, Leith Links.

1744– First published RULES OF GOLF. Honourable Company of Edinburgh Golfers.

1. You must tee your ball within a club's length of the hole.
2. Your tee must be upon the ground.
3. You are not to change the ball which you strike off the tee.
4. You are not to remove stones or bones for the sake of playing your ball, except upon the fair green and that only/within a club's length of your ball.
5. If your ball comes among water or any watery filth, you are at liberty to take out your ball and bringing it behind the hazard and teeing it, you may play it with any club and allow adversary a stroke for so getting out your ball.
6. If your balls be found anywhere touching one another, you are to lift the first ball, till you play the last.
7. At holling, you are to play your ball honestly for the hole and not to play upon your adversary's ball, not lying in your way to the hole.
8. If you should lose your ball, by it's being taken up or any other way, you are to go back to the spot where you struck last and

drop another ball, and allow your adversary a stroke for the misfortune.

9. No man at holling his ball is to be allowed to mark his way to the hole with his club or anything else.

10. If a ball be stopped by any person, horse, dog, or anything else, the ball so stopped must be played where it lies.

11. If you draw your club in order to strike and proceed so far in the stroke as to be accounted a stroke.

12. He whose ball lies farthest from the hole is obliged to play first.

13. Neither trench, ditch, or dyke made for the preservation of the links, nor the scholar's holes or the soldier's lines (uneven grounds) shall be accounted a hazard, but the ball is to be taken out teed/and played with any iron club.

1759– First stroke play event at St. Andrews, prior to this all play was match play.

1764– St. Andrews went from 22 to 18 holes, which became the standard. The front half at St. Andrews used to begin with four short holes, and the back half ended with four short holes. When this was the case, each half had eleven holes rather than the standard nine. In this year, they combined each of these short four holes into two longer holes, making the halves nine holes each, thus 18 holes total.

1766– The Blackheath Club is formed in London. The first golf club outside of Scotland.

1768– The first clubhouse in the world is built at Leith.

1774– The first year on the Old Club Cup, the oldest cup still played for, as proof of the first definite year of existence of the Royal Musselburgh Golf Club. Thomas McMillan won it and became the club's first Captain.

1786– The South Carolina Golf Club is formed. First outside the

United Kingdom and first in the United States.

1788– The Honourable Company of Edinburgh requires its members to wear uniforms while playing.

GOLF HISTORY – 1800's

1806– St. Andrews elects Captains rather than the Captain being the winner of their major tournament. Golf Club Captains deal with golf and social events that involve members. They also participate in a lot of the same things that a general manager or tournament director might be involved in.

1810– First formal women's tournament in the world held at Musselburgh.

1826– Hickory wood imported from the United States to make club shafts.

1833– St. Andrews bans stymies, but reverses itself the next year.

1834– William IV confers the title "ROYAL AND ANCIENT" to the St. Andrews Golf Club.

1836– Honourable Company of Edinburgh abandons the Leith golf course because of poor conditions. The Company moves to Musselburgh. St. Andrews replaces Leith as the most famous golf course as a result.

A Feathery ball is driven 361 yards, the longest drive in golf up to that point.

1848– The Gutta-Percha ball is created. Nicknamed the "Guttie." It is made from tree sap and is cheaper to make and goes further than the Feathery. This adds to the growth of golf.

1856– NEW RULE – Ball must be played as it lies.

1857– "THE GOLFERS MANUAL: BEING AN HISTORICAL AND DESCRIPTIVE ACCOUNT OF THE

NATIONAL GAME OF SCOTLAND" is published. First golf instruction book.

1858– The Royal Currach Golf Club is built in Kildare. The first club in Ireland.

Allan Robertson, recognized as the first great golf professional, is the first golfer to break 80 at St. Andrews. He shoots 79.

1860– The OPEN is created and played at Prestwick for the first several years. Willie Park Sr. is the winner.

1861– For the first time, amateurs are invited to play in the OPEN.

1867– First ladies golf club is formed at St. Andrews. The first club for women in the world.

1868– Young Tom Morris wins the first of four consecutive OPENS at age 17, the youngest OPEN Champion ever.

1870– Royal Adelaide Golf Club is formed. First in Australia.

Young Tom Morris wins his third OPEN in a row and thus gets permanent possession of the Challenge Belt.

1873– Royal Montreal Golf Club is formed. First in Canada, and the oldest active club in the United States and Canada.

St. Andrews hosts the OPEN for the first time.

1875– Young Tom Morris dies of grief after his wife and daughter die at childbirth. He was 24.

1881– Molds were made to create dimples in the gutta-percha ball. Golfers had discovered that the ball performed better after it was marked up than when it was smooth.

1888– A St. Andrews Golf Club was formed in the United States. Formed in 1888, it is the oldest remaining club in the United States. It is located in Hastings-on-Hudson, New York and was started thanks to a Scottish sportsman by the name of John Reid and a few of his friends. Their first interaction with the land that the club was built on was a fun game played on an improvised three holes. Their "clubhouse" was an apple tree that the men hung their coats on. Today, members of the club claim to be part of the "apple tree gang."

1890– The term BOGEY is introduced. At first, a bogey was the modern-day par, until the mid-1900's when it began to mean one over par.

1891– The Golfing Union of Ireland is formed. It is the oldest golf union in the world. This Union introduced its own handicapping system in which they used their most consistent player, Thomas Gilroy at the time, as a marker to base scores on and gave players of lesser ability a certain number of shots to match up their scores. This eventually developed into the first universal handicapping system.

Shinnecock Hills Golf Club is formed on Long Island.

1892– The Oakhurst Golf Club is founded in White Sulphur Springs, West Virginia. The Oakhurst Challenge is the oldest golf tournament in the United States, and its medal is the oldest golf prize.

First golf tournament with an admission charge. Prior to this money was raised by betting.

1893– First 18-hole course in the United States was built in Chicago. Originally a 9-hole course, Chicago Golf Club was expanded by founder Charles Blair Macdonald this year to become the first 18-hole golf course in all of North America. Two years later, the club moved to Wheaton, Illinois due to its popularity.

1894 – First OPEN held in England, at Royal St. George's Golf Club, and first time an Englishman man won.

USGA FORMED. Charter members are the Chicago Golf Club, The Country Club of Boston, Newport Country Club, St. Andrews Golf Club and Shinnecock Hills Golf Club.

1885– First United States Amateur is played. Charles Macdonald is the winner. The first United States Open is played the next day. Horace Rawlins is the winner. Both events were played at Newport GC in Newport, Rhode Island.

Van Cortlandt Golf Course opens in New York City. First public course in the United States.

The USGA bans using a pool cue as a putter.

1897– First NCAA golf championship is held. It was held at Ardsley Club in Ardsley-on-Hudson, New York. Louis Bayard Jr. of Princeton was the individual champion, while Yale won the team competition.
The first golf magazine in the United States, "GOLF," is published.

1898– The term BIRDIE is created at Atlantic Country Club.

The Royal Cinque Ports Golf Club is three miles from the Royal St. George Golf Club in Scotland, so, Freddie Tate made a bet that he could cover the distance in 40 shots or fewer. He put his 32nd shot through a window in the Cinque Ports clubhouse.

The Haskell golf ball is created by Coburn Haskell.

1899– The Western Open is played in Chicago. This is the fore-runner of the PGA Tour.

Chapter 10:
PGA TOUR HIGHLIGHTS BY YEAR

1860

MAJOR WINNERS

THE OPEN - Willie Park Sr., Prestwick (174)

Runner(s) Up: Tom Morris Sr. (176)

HIGHLIGHTS:

- Inaugural Open Championship.
- Eight Professional golfers competed.
- Prestwick was a 12-hole course at the time, so it was a one-day, three-round tournament.
- Prize given to the winner was the "Challenge Belt" made of Moroccan leather. The champion could keep the belt until the next OPEN was held.

1861

MAJOR WINNERS

THE OPEN - Tom Morris Sr., Prestwick (163)

Runner(s) Up: Willie Park Sr. (167)

HIGHLIGHTS:

- "Old" Tom Morris got his revenge against Park. Morris was the greenskeeper at Prestwick, so he had been upset about his loss in the first OPEN.
- First OPEN to host amateurs alongside the professionals.

1862

MAJOR WINNERS

THE OPEN - Tom Morris Sr., Prestwick (163)

Runner(s) Up: Willie Park Sr. (176)

HIGHLIGHTS:

- Winning by 13 strokes, Morris set a record for largest win margin ever recorded in THE OPEN that still stands today. Tiger Woods is the only golfer to have a larger margin recorded in a major, the U.S. OPEN in 2000 when he won by 15 strokes.
- Later in the year, embarrassed by his defeat, Park challenged Morris to an 8-round match, playing two rounds at each of the following courses: Musselburgh, Prestwick, North Berwick, and St. Andrews. He ended up losing to Morris by a total of 17 strokes over the course of those eight rounds.

1863

MAJOR WINNERS

THE OPEN - Willie Park Sr., Prestwick (168)

Runner(s) Up: Tom Morris Sr. (170)

HIGHLIGHTS:

- First year to have a purse (prize money to be split amongst the players). It was £10, but ended up being shared equally among the eight professionals that played (since amateurs are not allowed to accept financial prizes) instead of differing amounts based on how they placed.

- Park's brother, David Park, had been leading after the first round, but finished third. It was the first time anyone other than Morris or Willie Park Sr. appeared to contend.

1864

MAJOR WINNERS
THE OPEN - Tom Morris Sr., Prestwick (167)
Runner(s) Up: Andrew Strath (169)

HIGHLIGHTS:
- First time anyone other than Tom Morris Sr. or Willie Park Sr. finished in the top two.
- First time that winning THE OPEN came with a financial prize that was not split equally between the players. The champion received £6 and the Challenge Belt.
- In Westward Ho!, a village in England, the North Devon GC was founded.

1865

MAJOR WINNERS
THE OPEN - Andrew Strath, Prestwick (162)
Runner(s) Up: Willie Park Sr. (164)

HIGHLIGHTS:
- Strath was the first golfer to win that was not Morris or Park.
- That year, Strath had replaced Morris as the greenskeeper at

Prestwick because Morris had returned to St. Andrews, where he had gotten his start.

- Tom Morris Jr. (son of Morris Sr.) became the youngest known competitor at THE OPEN at 14 years and 147 days. Unfortunately, he withdrew in the third round due to poor play.
- This was the first year that official scorecards were used. Previously, any scrap of paper was used.

1866

MAJOR WINNERS

THE OPEN - Willie Park Sr., Prestwick (169)
Runner(s) Up: David Park (171)

HIGHLIGHTS:

- Willie Park Sr. led after every round, just as he did in the 1860 OPEN. Today, that is called going "wire-to-wire."
- One of only three times to have two brothers finish in the top-two at THE OPEN.
- Young Tom Morris Jr. finished the OPEN this year, finishing in ninth place, 18 strokes back.
- The London Scottish Golf Club was founded.

1867

MAJOR WINNERS

THE OPEN - Tom Morris Sr., Prestwick (170)
Runner(s) Up: Willie Park Sr. (172)

HIGHLIGHTS:

- With this win, Morris became the oldest OPEN Champion ever at 46 years and 102 days.

- Since it was a windy day, Morris used a wooden club with a flat face that they called a "driver-putter," which helped keep his ball under the wind. It can be said that it contributed to his victory that day.

- An amateur golfer made an impact in THE OPEN for the first time when William Doleman led the tournament after a first round 55 over the 12 holes.

1868

MAJOR WINNERS

THE OPEN - Tom Morris Jr., Prestwick (154)

Runner(s) Up: Tom Morris Sr. (157)

HIGHLIGHTS:

- Tom Morris Jr. already became the youngest competitor in THE OPEN in 1865, but this year, he became the youngest ever champion of THE OPEN at 17 years and 156 days.

- Each 12-hole round in this event set a new course record. Keep in mind that all three rounds (36 holes) were played on the same day. In the first round, it was Tom Morris Jr. with a 51, the second round was both Tom Morris Sr. and Willie Park Sr. with a pair of 50s, and in the final round, it was Tom Morris Jr. with a 49.

1869

MAJOR WINNERS
THE OPEN - Tom Morris Jr., Prestwick (157)
Runner(s) Up: Bob Kirk (168)

HIGHLIGHTS:
- THE OPEN's first ever hole-in-one was recorded by Tom Morris Jr. on the eighth hole in his first round.
- Yet, another OPEN that made it clear that Young Tom was going to be one of golf's greatest and perhaps the most dominant at the time.

1870

MAJOR WINNERS
THE OPEN - Tom Morris Jr., Prestwick (149)
Runner(s) Up: Bob Kirk (161)

HIGHLIGHTS:
- Being Morris Jr.'s third win in a row, he got to claim ownership of the Challenge Belt, as stated in the rules of THE OPEN.
- During his victory, Morris Jr. made the first ever three on Prestwick's first hole. In that day, they most likely would have labeled that 578-yard hole a par 6, so dunking that 200-yard shot was probably also the first ever albatross in THE OPEN.
- With a three on number one, it is easy to see how Morris Jr. broke the course record, yet again, with a first round 47.
- Morris' 36-hole total of 149 was the lowest ever while THE OPEN was played over 36 holes.

1871

MAJOR WINNERS

THE OPEN - None

Runner(s) Up - None

*No OPEN was played due to the lack of a new trophy to give out to the winner (see: 1870)

1872

MAJOR WINNERS

THE OPEN - Tom Morris Jr., Prestwick (166)

Runner(s) Up: Davie Strath (169)

HIGHLIGHTS:

- First and only time that someone has won THE OPEN four times in a row.
- Since Morris Jr. had the belt, and THE OPEN organizers had still not decided on a trophy, he received a medal. In fact, due to the failure of the quest for a new trophy, the tournament was only announced two days before it occurred, so it almost was not held two years in a row.
- St. Andrews and Musselburgh Links decided they, too, would host THE OPEN in a rotation.

1873

MAJOR WINNERS
THE OPEN - Tom Kidd, St. Andrews (179)
Runner(s) Up: Jamie Anderson (180)

HIGHLIGHTS:
- First year that the Champion received the Claret Jug. However, it was called the "Golf Champion Trophy" at the time. As with the Challenger Belt, the winner got to keep the trophy until the next OPEN.
- Even though Tom Kidd was the first to receive it, Tom Morris Jr. is the first name on it from 1872.
- The tournament was two, 18-hole rounds instead of three, 12-hole rounds since St. Andrews was 18 holes compared to Prestwick (St. Andrews was only nine holes, but it was played one way out and played the opposite coming in).
- Torrential rain caused the first ruling that dealt with moving a golf ball that was submerged in a puddle. Unlike today, moving the ball to a drier spot (no closer to the hole) cost a penalty stroke.

1874

MAJOR WINNERS
THE OPEN - Mungo Park, Musselburgh Links (159)
Runner(s) Up: Tom Morris Jr. (161)

HIGHLIGHTS:
- First year that Musselburgh Links hosted this Championship
- At Musselburgh, the tournament was four rounds of nine holes since it was a 9-hole course at the time.

- Mungo Park became the first rookie to ever win THE OPEN.
- The Park family (Mungo, his brother Willie Sr., etc.) used the motto "never up, never in" for putting, which can still be heard on a golf course today.

1875

MAJOR WINNERS

THE OPEN - Willie Park Sr., Prestwick (166)

Runner(s) Up: Bob Martin (168)

HIGHLIGHTS:

- Willie Park Sr.'s fourth and final win of THE OPEN since winning the first ever open in 1860.
- Neither Young Tom nor Old Tom Morris played in this OPEN because they were mourning the deaths of Young Tom's wife and child that died during childbirth. This was Young Tom's last opportunity to play in THE OPEN because he, too, died later in 1875.

1876

MAJOR WINNERS

THE OPEN - Bob Martin, St. Andrews (176)

Runner(s) Up: Davie Strath (176)

HIGHLIGHTS:

- This was the first time that two players had ever tied with the same score after 36 holes at THE OPEN. However, the first ever playoff did not occur this year. When Davie Strath failed to let the green clear on his 35th hole (the 17th), he hit one of the players in the group in front of him, but it also prevented his ball from going into the road. The Championship Committee struggled to decide on whether or not they should disqualify him, so, they wanted to see a 36-hole playoff the next day before making the decision. Strath refused to play in the playoff, arguing that they should make the ruling before proceeding with any sort of playoff. Since he failed to show up to the playoff, Martin won by default.

1877

MAJOR WINNERS
THE OPEN - Jamie Anderson, Musselburgh Links (160)
Runner(s) Up: Bob Pringle (162)

HIGHLIGHTS:
- This year began a new era of two dominant golfers, similar to the days of Tom Morris Sr. and Willie Park Sr. Their names were Jamie Anderson and Bob Ferguson.
- First of Anderson's three in a row.
- Anderson may have seemed like an underdog this year, as two other players attracted most of the crowd, Bob Ferguson and Davie Strath.

1878

MAJOR WINNERS

THE OPEN - Jamie Anderson, Prestwick (157)

Runner(s) Up: Bob Kirk (159)

HIGHLIGHTS:

- This was Anderson's most dramatic win. In the final round, he holed a full iron shot and had a hole-in-one on his 35th hole, to later win by only two. If he had not holed both, he probably would not have won outright, if at all.
- Before getting his hole-in-one, a spectator had told Anderson that he teed his ball outside of the teeing ground. Doing the right thing, he re-teed it correctly and got his hole-in-one. That lady may have saved Anderson from making a life-changing mistake.

1879

MAJOR WINNERS

THE OPEN - Jamie Anderson, St. Andrews (169)

Runner(s) Up: Andrew Kirkaldy, Jamie Allan (172)

HIGHLIGHTS:

- Anderson's third in a row, the best since Tom Morris' dominance in 1868-1872.
- Unlike his previous performance, Anderson's win this year was not so dramatic.
- Anderson did not have a chance to match Morris Jr.'s record the following year because he did not play in the 1880 OPEN for unknown reasons.

1880

MAJOR WINNERS

THE OPEN - Bob Ferguson, Musselburgh Links (162)

Runner(s) Up: Peter Paxton (167)

HIGHLIGHTS:

- This was Ferguson's home course and where he began caddying when he was just eight years old. It was also the course where he obtained his first of three OPEN victories in a row.
- As stated earlier, Anderson did not compete this year to go for four in a row. The April date of this year's OPEN was "not convenient" for him.

1881

MAJOR WINNERS

THE OPEN - Bob Ferguson, Prestwick (170)

Runner(s) Up: Jamie Anderson (173)

HIGHLIGHTS:

- This year's OPEN had horrendous weather with tremendous winds, rain, sleet, and even snow. Apparently, the storm killed almost 200 fisherman who were out to sea.
- Despite the weather, play was only delayed by an hour and a half. In today's world, the event would have been at least delayed until the next day. With 22 players in the field, only eight finished the event.

1882

MAJOR WINNERS

THE OPEN - Bob Ferguson, St. Andrews (171)

Runner(s) Up: Willie Fernie (174)

HIGHLIGHTS:

- Ferguson completed his hat-trick this year, despite not feeling like his form was where it should have been leading up to the event. He went on to fail at matching Young Tom Morris Jr.'s record of four in a row next year after a playoff loss.

- He was the last person to win three in a row until Peter Thomson in 1954-1956.

1883

MAJOR WINNERS

THE OPEN - Willie Fernie, Musselburgh Links (158)

Runner(s) Up: Bob Ferguson (158)

HIGHLIGHTS:

- This OPEN held the first ever playoff in an OPEN. The format was another 36-hole stroke play match held the next day.

- After 35 of the 36 playoff holes, Ferguson was up by one shot. A two-shot swing at the last hole left Fernie up a single shot over Ferguson, a devastating twist of fate. This would have been Ferguson's record-tying fourth win in a row and at his home course nonetheless.

- Simpsons Golf Shop at Carnoustie was established this year. It was founded by Robert Simpson, the brother of next year's champion, Jack Simpson. It is thought to be the second oldest golf shop ever, and it still stands, overlooking the 18th green at Carnoustie.

1884

MAJOR WINNERS

THE OPEN - Jack Simpson, Prestwick (160)
Runner(s) Up: Willie Fernie, Douglas Rolland (164)

HIGHLIGHTS:
- First year that Prestwick had been extended to be an 18-hole course, since it was previously only 12 holes.
- Jack Simpson was one of six golfing brothers, but was the only brother to win THE OPEN.

1885

MAJOR WINNERS

THE OPEN - Bob Martin, St. Andrews (171)
Runner(s) Up: Archie Simpson (172)
BRITISH AMATEUR - A. F. Mafie, Royal Liverpool (7&6)
Runner(s) Up: Horace Hutchinson

HIGHLIGHTS:
- Martin's second win at St. Andrews, which is a feat that very few have achieved.

- David Ayton, who finished third, had a five-stroke lead going into the 35th hole, but took an 11 on the hole. He ended up with a three-round total of 173, finishing only two strokes back. This was the second time that hole 17 was a huge factor in Martin's victory.

- First year of the British Amateur Championship. It was the idea of Secretary of Royal Liverpool GC, Thomas Owen Potter, to give the amateur players a championship. Only amateurs from recognized clubs could participate. He hoped that it would increase the popularity of golf and raise playing standards.

1886

MAJOR WINNERS
THE OPEN - David Brown, Musselburgh Links (157)
Runner(s) Up: Willie Campbell (159)
BRITISH AMATEUR - Horace Hutchinson, St. Andrews (7&6)
Runner(s) Up: Henry Lamb

HIGHLIGHTS:
- David Brown only really played THE OPEN when it came to Musselburgh because that is where he worked. However, after his success, he was more willing to travel to play elsewhere.

- At the time, Brown was not well known at all and surely was not any of the favorites to win THE OPEN that year.

1887

MAJOR WINNERS

THE OPEN - Willie Park Jr., Prestwick (161)

Runner(s) Up: Bob Martin (162)

BRITISH AMATEUR - Horace Hutchinson, Royal Liverpool (1 Up)

Runner(s) Up: John Ball Jr.

HIGHLIGHTS:

- Another son of another OPEN Champion. The Morris's and the Parks are the only two father-son duos to both win THE OPEN.
- Park Jr. never went in a single bunker over the 36 holes.
- In the first round, Willie Campbell (runner up in 1886) shot a course record 77, at least four strokes ahead of everyone else. On the 16th hole of his final round, appearing to have the win already wrapped up, he topped a drive into a fairway bunker and took four strokes to get out. That bunker was named "Willie Campbell's Grave," as he never did win an OPEN.

1888

MAJOR WINNERS

THE OPEN - Jack Burns, St. Andrews (171)

Runner(s) Up: Davie Anderson, Ben Sayers (172)

BRITISH AMATEUR - John Ball Jr., Prestwick (5&4)

Runner(s) Up: John E. Laidlay

HIGHLIGHTS:

- This OPEN also had an unusual ending. Jack Burns had thought that he tied with Anderson and Sayers at 172, leading to a three-way playoff the next day. However, a member of the Royal and Ancient Golf Club of St. Andrews who was checking the scorecard noticed an addition error. It turns out that Burns had shot a 46 instead of a 47 on his front nine of the first round, giving him a total of 171. Since players are only responsible for a correct hole-by-hole score, not the addition, Burns was deemed the winner of the 1888 OPEN by one stroke.

1889

MAJOR WINNERS

THE OPEN - Willie Park Jr., Musselburgh Links (155)
Runner(s) Up: Andrew Kirkaldy (155)
BRITISH AMATEUR - John E. Laidlay (2&1)
Runner(s) Up: Leslie M. Balfour

HIGHLIGHTS:

- Park Jr. and Kirkaldy both shot a 36-hole record low 155 at Musselburgh, but Park Jr. would go on to win by five strokes in the 36-hole playoff.
- Park Jr. inspired the saying, "a man who can putt is a match for anyone."
- This was the last OPEN held at Musselburgh, as the Honourable Company of Edinburgh Golfers moved to Muirfield in 1891, which subsequently hosted THE OPEN in 1892.

1890

MAJOR WINNERS

    THE OPEN - John Ball Jr., Prestwick (164)

    Runner(s) Up: Archie Simpson, Willie Fernie (167)

    BRITISH AMATEUR - John Ball Jr., Royal Liverpool (4&3)

    Runner(s) Up: John E. Laidlay

HIGHLIGHTS:

- John Ball Jr. was the first Englishman to win THE OPEN, but perhaps more importantly, the first amateur to win it.
- He was also the first of two amateurs to win THE OPEN and the BRITISH AMATEUR in the same year. Only Bobby Jones matched that in 1930.
- This was a big year for turning THE OPEN into an international event.

1891

MAJOR WINNERS

    THE OPEN - Hugh Kirkaldy, St. Andrews (166)

    Runner(s) Up: Andrew Kirkaldy, Willie Fernie (168)

    BRITISH AMATEUR - John E. Laidlay, St. Andrews (37 holes)

    Runner(s) Up: Harold Hilton

HIGHLIGHTS:

- Hugh Kirkaldy's 166 was a record for THE OPEN at St. Andrews while it was contested over 36 holes.
- Andrew Kirkaldy, who never did win an OPEN, finished runner up for a third time, beaten by his own younger brother.
- This was the last year that THE OPEN was 36 holes in one day.

1892

MAJOR WINNERS

THE OPEN - Harold Hilton, Muirfield (305)
Runner(s) Up: Hugh Kirkaldy, John Ball Jr., Sandy Herd (308)
BRITISH AMATEUR - John Ball Jr., Royal St. George's (3 & 1)
Runner(s) Up: Harold Hilton

HIGHLIGHTS:

- The first four round, 72-hole OPEN. It was played over only two days, 36 holes each day.
- Muirfield was the new home of the Honourable Company of Edinburgh Golfers, which used to be hosted by Musselburgh Links. That is why it replaced Musselburgh as the third leg of the rotation of golf courses that hosted THE OPEN.
- Hilton was almost unable to play because his father was reluctant to give him time off from working the family business.

1893

MAJOR WINNERS

THE OPEN - Willie Auchterlonie, Prestwick (322)
Runner(s) Up: John E. Laidlay (324)
BRITISH AMATEUR - Peter Anderson, Prestwick (1 Up)
Runner(s) Up: John E. Laidlay

HIGHLIGHTS:

- Another year that had terrible weather conditions. On the first day, it poured from dawn to dusk. Old Tom Morris, who was playing in his 31st OPEN, said it was the worst weather he had ever played in.

- This year's prize money for the Champion showed signs of THE OPEN gaining more attention and importance. It was £30, which was more than the entire purse was only two years prior.

1894

MAJOR WINNERS

THE OPEN - John Henry "J.H." Taylor, Royal St. George's (326)
Runner(s) Up: Douglas Rolland (331)
BRITISH AMATEUR - John Ball Jr., Royal Liverpool (1 Up)
Runner(s) Up: S. Mure Fergusson

HIGHLIGHTS:

- First OPEN held outside of Scotland since Royal St. George's is in England.
- Although there was fear that there would not be many players due to the location, a 94-player starting field was a record for the time.
- This was the year that began two decades of dominance by three professionals: J.H. Taylor, Harry Vardon, and James Braid. They won 16 OPENs in 20 years.

1895

*MAJOR WINNERS:

U.S. OPEN – Horace Rawlins, Newport Golf Club (173)
Runner(s) Up: Willie Dunn (175)

THE OPEN – John Henry "J.H." Taylor, St. Andrews (322)
Runner(s) Up: Alex "Sandy" Herd (326)
**U.S. AMATEUR – Charles Macdonald, Newport GC (12&11)
Runner(s) Up: Charles Sands
BRITISH AMATEUR – Leslie Balfour-Melville, St. Andrews (19 holes)
Runner(s) Up: John Ball Jr.

HIGHLIGHTS:

- Inaugural U.S. Open and U.S. Amateur
- The U.S. Open was contested over 36 holes until 1898, when it extended to 72 holes.
- Spalding becomes the first American company to manufacture golf balls.
- The pool cue is banned as a putter by the USGA.

*Before the inaugural Masters tournament, both Open and Amateur Championships were considered the four majors
**U.S. Amateur was match play 1895-1964

1896

MAJOR WINNERS:

U.S. OPEN – James Foulis, Shinnecock Hills (152)
Runner(s) Up: Horace Rawlins (155)
THE OPEN – Harry Vardon, Muirfield (316)
Runner(s) Up: J.H. Taylor (316)
U.S. AMATEUR – H.J. Whigham, Shinnecock Hills (8&7)
Runner(s) Up: J.G. Thorp
BRITISH AMATEUR – Freddie Tait, Royal St. Georges (8&7)
Runner(s) Up: Harold Hilton

HIGHLIGHTS:

- Harry Vardon wins his first of six Open Championships in a 36-hole playoff over J.H. Taylor, 157-161.
- "The Game of Golf" is written and published by Willie Park, Jr., an Open Championship winner along with being a golf course designer and club maker.

1897

MAJOR WINNERS:

U.S. OPEN – Joe Lloyd, Chicago Golf Club (162)
Runner(s) Up: Willie Anderson (163)
THE OPEN – Harold Hilton, Royal Liverpool (314)
Runner(s) Up: James Braid (315)
U.S. AMATEUR – H.J. Whigham, Chicago Golf Club (8&6)
Runner(s) Up: W. Rossiter Betts
BRITISH AMATEUR – Jack Allan, Muirfield (4&2)
Runner(s) Up: James Robb

HIGHLIGHTS:

- Yale University wins the first collegiate golf tournament played in the U.S.
- President McKinley tries golf during a vacation, becoming the first sitting President to play the game.
- MacGregor Golf markets its first clubs.

1898

MAJOR WINNERS:

U.S. OPEN – Fred Herd, Myopia Hunt Club (328)

Runner(s) Up: Alex Smith (335)

THE OPEN – Harry Vardon, Prestwick GC (307)

Runner(s) Up: Willie Park Jr. (308)

U.S. AMATEUR – Findlay S. Douglas, Morris County GC (5&3)

Runner(s) Up: Walter Smith

BRITISH AMATEUR – Freddie Tait, Royal Liverpool (7&5)

Runner(s) Up: Samuel "S" Mure Fergusson

HIGHLIGHTS:

- The U.S. Open expands from 36 holes in one day to 72 holes in two days.
- The term "birdie" is introduced.
- The Open Championship introduces a 36-hole cut.

1899

MAJOR WINNERS:

U.S. OPEN – Willie Smith, Baltimore CC (315)

Runner(s) Up: Val Fitzjohn, George Low Sr., William Herbert "Bert" Way (326)

THE OPEN – Harry Vardon, Royal St. Georges (310)

Runner(s) Up: Jack White (315)

U.S. AMATEUR – H.M. Harriman, Onwentsia Club (3&2)

Runner(s) Up: Findlay S. Douglas

BRITISH AMATEUR – John Ball Jr., Prestwick GC (37 holes)

Runner(s) Up: Freddie Tait

HIGHLIGHTS:

- The Western Open is played for the first time, the first tournament in what would evolve into the PGA Tour.
- Donald Ross, a legendary golf course designer, serves as greenskeeper apprentice to Old Tom Morris at St. Andrews.

1900

MAJOR WINNERS:

U.S. OPEN – Harry Vardon, Chicago GC, (313)
Runner(s) Up: J.H. Taylor (315)
THE OPEN – J.H. Taylor, St. Andrews (309)
Runner(s) Up: Harry Vardon (317)
U.S. AMATEUR – Walter Travis, Garden City GC (2 up)
Runner(s) Up: Findlay S. Douglas
BRITISH AMATEUR – Harold Hilton, Royal St. Georges (8&7)
Runner(s) Up: James Robb

HIGHLIGHTS:

- J.H. Taylor, Harry Vardon, and James Braid, known as the "Great Triumvirate," finish 1-2-3 in the Open Championship.
- Harry Vardon, touring the U.S. on an exhibition, wins the U.S. Open, and his tour is credited with generating interest in golf in America.
- Haskell balls are mass produced, while gutta-percha balls fade in use.

<h1 style="text-align:center">1901</h1>

MAJOR WINNERS:

U.S. OPEN – Willie Anderson, Myopia Hunt Club (331)

Runner(s) Up: Alex Smith (331)

THE OPEN – James Braid, Muirfield (309)

Runner(s) Up: Harry Vardon (312)

U.S. AMATEUR – Walter Travis, CC of Atlantic City (5&4)

Runner(s) Up: Walter Egan

BRITISH AMATEUR – Harold Hilton, St. Andrews (1 up)

Runner(s) Up: John Low

HIGHLIGHTS:

- Willie Anderson wins the U.S. Open in a playoff over Alex Smith, 85-86.
- The first nine holes of future Pinehurst No. 2 open.
- Walter Travis becomes the first to win a major using a wound, rubber-core ball, otherwise known as a Haskell.

<h1 style="text-align:center">1902</h1>

MAJOR WINNERS:

U.S. OPEN – Laurie Auchterlonie, Garden City GC (307)

Runner(s) Up: Stewart Gardner, Walter Travis (313)

THE OPEN – Sandy Herd, Royal Liverpool (307)

Runner(s) Up: James Braid, Harry Vardon (308)

U.S. AMATEUR – Louis James, Glen View Club (4&2)

Runner(s) Up: Eben Byers

BRITISH AMATEUR – Charles Hutchings, Royal Liverpool (1 up)

Runner(s) Up: Sidney Fry

HIGHLIGHTS:

- Willie Anderson is the first player to break 300 in a U.S. tournament, shooting 299 in the Western Open.
- A Haskell ball is used by Sandy Herd in his victory in the Open Championship. A Haskell flew further than a gutta-percha ball and so became the standard.

1903

MAJOR WINNERS:

U.S. OPEN – Willie Anderson, Baltusrol GC (307)

Runner(s) Up: David Brown (307)

THE OPEN – Harry Vardon, Prestwick GC (300)

Runner(s) Up: Tom Vardon (306)

U.S. AMATEUR – Walter Travis, CC of Atlantic City (5 & 4)

Runner(s) Up: Eben Byers

BRITISH AMATEUR – Robert Maxwell, Muirfield (7 & 5)

Runner(s) Up: Horace Hutchinson

HIGHLIGHTS:

- Willie Anderson wins the U.S. Open in an 18-hole playoff over David Brown, 82-84.
- A 9-hole golf course is built in Kobe, Japan, becoming the first course in Japan.
- Oakmont Country Club opens.
- Balata covers are now used as the cover material on a golf ball as opposed to the less durable gutta-percha.

1904

MAJOR WINNERS:

U.S. OPEN – Willie Anderson, Glen View Club (303)

Runner(s) Up: Gil Nicholls (308)

THE OPEN – Jack White, Royal St. Georges (296)

Runner(s) Up: James Braid, J.H. Taylor (297)

U.S. AMATEUR – H. Chandler Egan, Baltusrol GC (8&6)

Runner(s) Up: Fred Herreshoff

BRITISH AMATEUR – Walter Travis, Royal St. Georges (4&3)

Runner(s) Up: Edward Blackwell

HIGHLIGHTS:

- James Braid becomes the first to break 70 in the Open Championship, shooting a 69 in the third round, but J.H. Taylor and Jack White shoot 68 and 69 in the final round. White wins, and his 296 makes him the first to break 300 in the Open.
- Walter Travis is the first U.S. Citizen to win the British Amateur.
- Golf is included in the Olympics for the second time.

1905

MAJOR WINNERS:

U.S. OPEN – Willie Anderson, Baltusrol GC (314)

Runner(s) Up: Alex Smith (316)

THE OPEN – James Braid, St. Andrews (318)

Runner(s) Up: Rowland Jones, J.H. Taylor (323)

U.S. AMATEUR – H. Chandler Egan, Chicago GC (6&5)

Runner(s) Up: D.E. Sawyer

BRITISH AMATEUR – Arthur Barry, Prestwick GC (3&2)

Runner(s) Up: Osmund Scott

HIGHLIGHTS:
- Dimples first appear on golf balls.
- Harry Vardon's golf book, "The Complete Golfer," is published.
- Willie Anderson becomes the first player to win the U.S. Open four times and is still the only to win three straight.

1906

MAJOR WINNERS:

U.S. OPEN – Alex Smith, Onwentsia Club (295)
Runner(s) Up: Willie Smith (302)
THE OPEN – James Braid, Muirfield (300)
Runner(s) Up: J.H. Taylor (304)
U.S. AMATEUR – Eben Byers, Englewood GC (2 up)
Runner(s) Up: George Lyon
BRITISH AMATEUR – James Robb, Royal Liverpool (4&3)
Runner(s) Up: C.C. Lingen

HIGHLIGHTS:
- Alex Smith is the first player to break 300 in the U.S. Open.

1907

MAJOR WINNERS:

U.S. OPEN – Alec Ross, Philadelphia Cricket Club (302)
Runner(s) Up: Gil Nicholls (304)
THE OPEN – Arnaud Massy, Royal Liverpool (312)

Runner(s) Up: J.H. Taylor (314)

U.S. AMATEUR – Jerome Travers, Euclid Club (6&5)

Runner(s) Up: Archibald Graham

BRITISH AMATEUR – John Ball, St. Andrews (6&4)

Runner(s) Up: C.A. Palmer

HIGHLIGHTS:

- Arnaud Massy becomes the first and still only Frenchman to win the Open Championship.

1908

MAJOR WINNERS:

U.S. OPEN – Fred McLeod, Myopia Hunt Club (322)

Runner(s) Up: Willie Smith (322)

THE OPEN – James Braid, Prestwick GC (291)

Runner(s) Up: Tom Ball (299)

U.S. AMATEUR – Jerome Travers, Garden City GC (8&7)

Runner(s) Up: Max Behr

BRITISH AMATEUR – E.A. Lassen, Royal St. Georges (7&6)

Runner(s) Up: H.E. Taylor

HIGHLIGHTS:

- Fred McLeod wins the U.S. Open in a playoff over Willie Smith, 77-83

  *FROM 1908 BACK (US OPEN), RELATION TO PAR WAS UNAVAILABLE

1909

MAJOR WINNERS:

U.S. OPEN – George Sargent, Englewood GC (+2)

Runner(s) Up: Tom McNamara (+6)

THE OPEN – J.H. Taylor, Royal Cinque Ports (295)

Runner(s) Up: Tom Ball, James Braid (301)

U.S. AMATEUR – Robert Gardner, Chicago GC (4&3)

Runner(s) Up: H. Chandler Egan

BRITISH AMATEUR – Robert Maxwell, Muirfield (1 up)

Runner(s) Up: C.K. Hutchison

HIGHLIGHTS:

* David Hunter posts the first sub-70 round in a U.S. Open with a 68.

1910

MAJOR WINNERS:

U.S. OPEN – Alex Smith, Philadelphia Cricket Club (+6)

Runner(s) Up: John McDermott, Macdonald Smith (+6)

THE OPEN – James Braid, St. Andrews (299)

Runner(s) Up: Alex Herd (303)

U.S. AMATEUR – William Fownes Jr., The Country Club (Brookline) (4&3)

Runner(s) Up: Warren Wood

BRITISH AMATEUR – John Ball, Royal Liverpool (10&9)

Runner(s) Up: C.C. Aylmer

HIGHLIGHTS:

* Alex Smith wins the U.S. Open over 18-year-old John McDer-

mott and his brother Macdonald Smith in an 18-hole playoff, shooting 71 to their 75 and 77, respectively.

- Steel shafted clubs begin development by Arthur Knight

1911

MAJOR WINNERS:

U.S. OPEN – John McDermott, Chicago GC (+3)

Runner(s) Up: Mike Brady, George Simpson (+3)

THE OPEN – Harry Vardon, Royal St. Georges (303)

Runner(s) Up: Arnaud Massy (303)

U.S. AMATEUR – Harold Hilton, The Apawamis Club (37 holes)

Runner(s) Up: Fred Herreshoff

BRITISH AMATEUR – Harold Hilton, Prestwick GC (4&3)

Runner(s) Up: E.A. Lassen

HIGHLIGHTS:

- John McDermott becomes the first American born player and the youngest ever winner of the U.S. Open at age 19, a record which stills stands today. He wins in a playoff over Mike Brady and George Simpson, shooting 80 to their 82 and 85 respectively.

- Harold Hilton is the first foreign born player to win the U.S. Amateur. Also the first to win the U.S. and British Amateurs in the same year.

- Harry Vardon wins the Open Championship in a playoff over Arnaud Massy, shooting 138 to Massy's 148. Although the playoff was supposed to go 36 holes, the pair only finished 34 of them. Massy conceded after Vardon had reached the 17th hole (par 4 playing straight into the wind) in two shots. Massy was ten strokes back at that point, thus he had enough.

1912

MAJOR WINNERS:

U.S. OPEN – John McDermott, CC of Buffalo (+6)
Runner(s) Up: Tom McNamara (+8)
THE OPEN – Ted Ray, Muirfield (295)
Runner(s) Up: Harry Vardon (299)
U.S. AMATEUR – Jerome Travers, Chicago GC (7&6)
Runner(s) Up: Chick Evans
BRITISH AMATEUR – John Ball, Royal North Devon (38 holes)
Runner(s) Up: Abe Mitchell

HIGHLIGHTS:

- John Ball wins his record eighth British Amateur championship, a record which still stands for most wins in a single major. (At the time, this was considered a major championship)
- John McDermott, upon winning his second straight U.S. Open, becomes the first golfer to shoot under par in a single round of the event.
- Ben Hogan, Byron Nelson, and Sam Snead are all born, and all within months of each other.

1913

MAJOR WINNERS:

U.S. OPEN – Francis Ouimet (a), The Country Club (Brookline) (+12)

Runner(s) Up: Ted Ray, Harry Vardon (+12)

THE OPEN – J.H. Taylor, Royal Liverpool (304)

Runner(s) Up: Ted Ray (312)

U.S. AMATEUR – Jerome Travers, Garden City GC (5&4)

Runner(s) Up: John Anderson

BRITISH AMATEUR – Harold Hilton, St. Andrews (6&5)

Runner(s) Up: Robert Harris

HIGHLIGHTS:

- At age 20, Francis Ouimet becomes the first amateur to win the U.S. Open. His defeat of British greats Harry Vardon and Ted Ray in a playoff becomes highly publicized and is known as one of golf's most famous upsets. Ouimet shoots 72 to Vardon's 77 and Ray's 78. A movie was filmed in 2005, titled "The Greatest Game Ever Played," and it was a recreation of this match and the events leading up to it.
- Ouimet's caddie, Edward Edgar Lowery, was ten years old. As he grew up, he, too, was a golfer, but remained an amateur. He would go on to become a multi-millionaire as a car dealer.

1914

MAJOR WINNERS:

U.S. OPEN – Walter Hagen, Midlothian CC (+2)

Runner(s) Up: Chick Evans (+3)

*THE OPEN – Harry Vardon, Prestwick GC (306)

Runner(s) Up: J.H. Taylor (309)

U.S. AMATEUR – Francis Ouimet, Ekwanok CC (6&5)

Runner(s) Up: Jerome Travers
BRITISH AMATEUR – J.L.C. Jenkins, Royal St. Georges (3&2)
Runner(s) Up: Charles Hezlet

HIGHLIGHTS:
- Harry Vardon wins his sixth Open Championship, a record to this day.
- Francis Ouimet becomes the first golfer with victories in both the U.S. Open and U.S. Amateur upon his victory over Jerome Travers in the U.S. Amateur final.
- Walter Hagen wins his first U.S. Open, becoming the first to do so in wire-to-wire fashion.
  *From 1914 Back (OPEN Championship), to par was unavailable

1915

MAJOR WINNERS:
U.S. OPEN – Jerome Travers (a), Baltusrol GC (+1)
Runner(s) Up: Tom McNamara (+2)
THE OPEN – None due to WWI
U.S. AMATEUR – Robert Gardner, CC of Detroit (5&4)
Runner(s) Up: John Anderson
BRITISH AMATEUR – None due to WWI

HIGHLIGHTS:
- Open Championship discontinued for the rest of WWI.
- Travers won his first and only U.S. OPEN after winning the U.S. Amateur four times. He retired shortly after this win.

1916

MAJOR WINNERS:

U.S. OPEN – Chick Evans (a), Minikahda Club (-2)

Runner(s) Up: Jock Hutchison (E)

THE OPEN – None due to WWI

*PGA CHAMPIONSHIP – James Barnes, Siwanoy CC (1 up)

Runner(s) Up: Jock Hutchison

U.S. AMATEUR – Chick Evans, Merion Cricket Club (4&3)

Runner(s) Up: Robert Gardner

BRITISH AMATEUR – None due to WWI

HIGHLIGHTS:

- *Inaugural PGA Championship, not yet considered a major when speaking of Grand Slams, but a major golf tournament nonetheless (important for 1930).
- Chick Evans pulls off a wire-to-wire victory in the U.S. Open and sets a new scoring record. Not bad for his only U.S. Open victory. Also he becomes the first to win both the U.S. Open and U.S. Amateur in the same year.
- The Professional Golfers Association is founded.
- At age 14 and playing in his first U.S. Amateur, Bobby Jones makes it to the quarterfinals.

1917

MAJOR WINNERS:

U.S. OPEN – None due to WWI

THE OPEN – None due to WWI

PGA CHAMPIONSHIP – None due to WWI

U.S. AMATEUR – None due to WWI

BRITISH AMATEUR – None due to WWI

*During this time, no matches were played because of World War I.

1918

MAJOR WINNERS:

U.S. OPEN – None due to WWI

THE OPEN – None due to WWI

PGA CHAMPIONSHIP – None due to WWI

U.S. AMATEUR – None due to WWI

BRITISH AMATEUR – None due to WWI

*No championships due to WWI

1919

MAJOR WINNERS:

U.S. OPEN – Walter Hagen, Brae Burn CC (+17)

Runner(s) Up: Mike Brady (+17)

THE OPEN – None due to WWI

PGA CHAMPIONSHIP – James Barnes, Engineers CC (6&5)

Runner(s) Up: Fred McLeod

U.S. AMATEUR – Davidson Herron, Oakmont CC (5&4)

Runner(s) Up: Bobby Jones

BRITISH AMATEUR – None due to WWI

HIGHLIGHTS:

- Walter Hagen wins the U.S. Open in a playoff over Mike Brady, winning by one stroke in an 18-hole playoff, 77-78.

- Pebble Beach Golf Links opens.
- The U.S. Open is played over three days for the first time, 18 the first two days, and 36 the final.

1920

MAJOR WINNERS:

U.S. OPEN – Ted Ray, Inverness Club (+7)

Runner(s) Up: Jack Burke Sr., Leo Diegel, Jock Hutchison, Harry Vardon (+8)

THE OPEN – George Duncan, Royal Cinque Ports (+15)

Runner(s) Up: Alex Herd (+17)

PGA CHAMPIONSHIP – Jock Hutchison, Flossmoor CC (1 up)

Runner(s) Up: J. Douglas Edgar

U.S. AMATEUR – Chick Evans, Engineers CC (7&6)

Runner(s) Up: Francis Ouimet

BRITISH AMATEUR – Cyril Tolley, Muirfield (37 holes)

Runner(s) Up: Robert Gardner

HIGHLIGHTS:

- "The Professional Golfer in America" is first published. Today it is the oldest continually-published golf magazine, better known as the "PGA Magazine."
- Britain resumes its tournaments following WWI.

1921

MAJOR WINNERS:

U.S. OPEN – James Barnes, Columbia CC (+9)

Runner(s) Up: Walter Hagen, Fred McLeod (+18)

THE OPEN – Jock Hutchison, St. Andrews (+8)

Runner(s) Up: Roger Wethered (a) (+8)

PGA CHAMPIONSHIP – Walter Hagen, Inwood CC (3&2)

Runner(s) Up: James Barnes

U.S. AMATEUR – Jesse Guilford, St. Louis CC (7&6)

Runner(s) Up: Robert Gardner

BRITISH AMATEUR – Willie Hunter, Royal Liverpool (12&11)

Runner(s) Up: Allan Graham

HIGHLIGHTS:

- Jock Hutchison wins the Open Championship in a playoff over amateur Roger Wethered in a 36-hole playoff. It was Hutchison's second and final major.
- George H. Walker, great-grandfather to President George W. Bush, donates the "International Challenge Trophy" for an amateur event, later known as the Walker Cup.

1922

MAJOR WINNERS:

U.S. OPEN – Gene Sarazen, Skokie CC (+8)

Runner(s) Up: John Black, Bobby Jones (a) (+9)

THE OPEN – Walter Hagen, Royal St. Georges (+20)

Runner(s) Up: James Barnes, George Duncan (+21)

PGA CHAMPIONSHIP – Gene Sarazen, Oakmont CC (4&3)

Runner(s) Up: Emmet French

U.S. AMATEUR – Jess Sweetser, The Country Club (3&2)
Runner(s) Up: Chick Evans
BRITISH AMATEUR – Ernest Holderness, Prestwick GC (1 up)
Runner(s) Up: John Caven

HIGHLIGHTS:

- Gene Sarazen becomes the first to win both the U.S. Open and PGA Championship in the same year.
- The first Walker Cup matches are held.
- Walter Hagen becomes the first golfer to begin a golf equipment company under his own name.

1923

MAJOR WINNERS:

U.S. OPEN – Bobby Jones (a), Inwood CC (+8)
Runner(s) Up: Bobby Cruikshank (+8)
THE OPEN – Arthur Havers, Royal Troon (+7)
Runner(s) Up: Walter Hagen (+8)
PGA CHAMPIONSHIP – Gene Sarazen, Pelham CC (38 holes)
Runner(s) Up: Walter Hagen
U.S. AMATEUR – Max Marston, Flossmoor CC (38 holes)
Runner(s) Up: Jess Sweetser
BRITISH AMATEUR – Roger Wethered, Royal Cinque Ports (7&6)
Runner(s) Up: Robert Harris

HIGHLIGHTS:

- Bobby Jones defeats Bobby Cruikshank to win his first major at the U.S. Open, shooting 76 in an 18-hole playoff to Cruikshank's 78.

- Walter Hagen records a 62 at the Florida West Coast Championship, the lowest round in a pro tournament at this point.

1924

MAJOR WINNERS:

U.S. OPEN – Cyril Walker, Oakland Hills (+9)
Runner(s) Up: Bobby Jones (a) (+12)
THE OPEN – Walter Hagen, Royal Liverpool (+13)
Runner(s) Up: Ernest Whitcombe (+14)
PGA CHAMPIONSHIP – Walter Hagen, French Lick Springs GC (2 up)
Runner(s) Up: James Barnes
U.S. AMATEUR – Bobby Jones, Merion Cricket Club (9&8)
Runner(s) Up: George Von Elm
BRITISH AMATEUR – Ernest Holderness, St. Andrews (3&2)
Runner(s) Up: E.F. Storey

HIGHLIGHTS:
USGA rules steel shafted clubs legal.
Walter Hagen wins the first of four straight PGA Championships
Sectional qualifying for the U.S. Open is introduced.

1925

MAJOR WINNERS:

U.S. OPEN – Willie MacFarlane, Worcester CC (+7)
Runner(s) Up: Bobby Jones (a) (+7)
THE OPEN – James Barnes, Prestwick GC (+16)
Runner(s) Up: Archie Compston, Ted Ray (+17)

PGA CHAMPIONSHIP – Walter Hagen, Olympia Fields (6&5)

Runner(s) Up: William Mehlhorn

U.S. AMATEUR – Bobby Jones, Oakmont CC (8&7)

Runner(s) Up: Watts Gunn

BRITISH AMATEUR – Robert Harris, Royal North Devon (13&12)

Runner(s) Up: Kenneth F. Fradgley

HIGHLIGHTS:

- Willie MacFarlane defeats Bobby Jones in a 36-hole playoff by one stroke to win the U.S. Open.
- The Open Championship is played for the final time at Prestwick GC.

1926

MAJOR WINNERS:

U.S. OPEN – Bobby Jones (a), Scioto CC (+5)

Runner(s) Up: Joe Turnesa (+6)

THE OPEN – Bobby Jones (a), Royal Lytham & St. Annes (+7)

Runner(s) Up: Al Watrous (+9)

PGA CHAMPIONSHIP – Walter Hagen, Salisbury GL (5&3)

Runner(s) Up: Leo Diegel

U.S. AMATEUR – George Von Elm, Baltusrol GC (2&1)

Runner(s) Up: Bobby Jones

BRITISH AMATEUR – Jess Sweetser, Muirfield (6&5)

Runner(s) Up: A.F. Simpson

HIGHLIGHTS:

- Bobby Jones becomes the first to win both the U.S. Open and Open Championship in the same year.

- Los Angeles Open is the first event to offer a purse of at least $10,000, to be split up amongst the top finishers

1927

MAJOR WINNERS:

U.S. OPEN – Tommy Armour, Oakmont CC (+13)
Runner(s) Up: Harry Cooper (+13)
THE OPEN – Bobby Jones (a), St. Andrews (-7)
Runner(s) Up: Aubrey Boomer, Fred Robson (-1)
PGA CHAMPIONSHIP – Walter Hagen, Cedar Crest CC (1 up)
Runner(s) Up: Joe Turnesa
U.S. AMATEUR – Bobby Jones, Minikahda Club (8&7)
Runner(s) Up: Chick Evans
BRITISH AMATEUR – William Tweddell, Royal Liverpool (7&6)
Runner(s) Up: D.E. Landale

HIGHLIGHTS:

- Tommy Armour wins the U.S. Open in an 18-hole playoff over Harry Cooper, 76-79.
- Inaugural Ryder Cup matches are held, with the U.S. defeating Great Britain 9.5-2.5.

1928

MAJOR WINNERS:

U.S. OPEN – Johnny Farrell, Olympia Fields (+10)
Runner(s) Up: Bobby Jones (a) (+10)

THE OPEN – Walter Hagen, Royal St. Georges (+12)

Runner(s) Up: Gene Sarazen (+14)

PGA CHAMPIONSHIP – Leo Diegel, Five Farms CC (6&5)

Runner(s) Up: Al Espinosa

U.S. AMATEUR – Bobby Jones, Brae Burn CC (10&9)

Runner(s) Up: Philip Perkins

BRITISH AMATEUR – Philip Perkins, Prestwick GC (6&4)

Runner(s) Up: Roger Wethered

HIGHLIGHTS:

- Johnny Farrell wins the U.S. Open over Bobby Jones in a 36-hole playoff, 143-144. The driver he used featured a metal clubhead.

1929

MAJOR WINNERS:

U.S. OPEN – Bobby Jones (a), Winged Foot GC (+6)

Runner(s) Up: Al Espinosa (+6)

THE OPEN – Walter Hagen, Muirfield (+8)

Runner(s) Up: Johnny Farrell (+14)

PGA CHAMPIONSHIP – Leo Diegel, Hillcrest CC (6&4)

Runner(s) Up: Johnny Farrell

U.S. AMATEUR – Harrison Johnston, Del Monte Golf & Country Club (4&3)

Runner(s) Up: O.F. Willing

BRITISH AMATEUR – Cyril Tolley, Royal St. Georges (4&3)

Runner(s) Up: J. Nelson Smith

- Bobby Jones wins the U.S. Open in a 36-hole playoff over Al Espinosa, which Jones wins by 23 strokes.
- Steel shafts are legalized by the R&A.

1930

MAJOR WINNERS:

U.S. OPEN – Bobby Jones (a), Interlachen CC (-1)
Runner(s) Up: Macdonald Smith (+1)
THE OPEN – Bobby Jones (a), Royal Liverpool (+3)
Runner(s) Up: Leo Diegel, Macdonald Smith (+5)
PGA CHAMPIONSHIP – Tommy Armour, Fresh Meadows CC (1 up)
Runner(s) Up: Gene Sarazen
U.S. AMATEUR – Bobby Jones, Merion Cricket Club (8&7)
Runner(s) Up: Eugene Homans
BRITISH AMATEUR – Bobby Jones, St. Andrews (7&6)
Runner(s) Up: Roger Wethered

HIGHLIGHTS

- Bobby Jones won all four "major" golf tournaments (at the time) this year, completing the first and only "Grand Slam."
- Bobby Jones also retired from competitive golf this year, at just age 28.

1931

MAJOR WINNERS:

U.S. OPEN – Billy Burke, Inverness Club (+8)

Runner(s) Up: George Von Elm (+8)

THE OPEN – Tommy Armour, Carnoustie (+12)

Runner(s) Up: Jose Jurado (+13)

PGA CHAMPIONSHIP – Tom Creavy, Wannamoisett CC (2&1)

Runner(s) Up: Denny Shute

U.S. AMATEUR – Francis Ouimet, Beverly CC (6&5)

Runner(s) Up: Jack Westland

BRITISH AMATEUR – Eric Martin-Smith, Royal North Devon (1 up)

Runner(s) Up: John DeForest

HIGHLIGHTS

- Billy Burke won the U.S. OPEN in a stunning 72-hole playoff. They were both still tied after the first 36 playoff holes, so they had to play another 36 the next day.
- Bobby Jones bought the plot of land that Augusta National Golf Club would eventually be built on.
- First year of sectional qualifying for the U.S. Amateur.

1932

MAJOR WINNERS:

U.S. OPEN – Gene Sarazen, Fresh Meadow CC (+6)

Runner(s) Up: Bobby Cruikshank, Phil Perkins (+9)

THE OPEN – Gene Sarazen, Prince's Golf Club (-5)

Runner(s) Up: Macdonald Smith (E)

PGA CHAMPIONSHIP – Olin Dutra, Keller GC (4&3)

Runner(s) Up: Frank Walsh

U.S. AMATEUR – Ross Somerville, Baltimore CC (2&1)

Runner(s) Up: John Goodman

BRITISH AMATEUR – John DeForest, Muirfield (3&1)

Runner(s) Up: Eric Fiddian

HIGHLIGHTS

- Gene Sarazen became the second man (besides Bobby Jones) to win the U.S. and British Open in the same year.
- First ever Curtis Cup is held, also named "The Women's International Cup." The U.S. won against Great Britain and Ireland.

1933

MAJOR WINNERS:

U.S. OPEN – John Goodman (a), North Shore CC (-1)

Runner(s) Up: Ralph Guldahl (E)

THE OPEN – Denny Shute, St. Andrews (E)

Runner(s) Up: Craig Wood (E)

PGA CHAMPIONSHIP – Gene Sarazen, Blue Mound CC (5&4)

Runner(s) Up: Willie Goggin

U.S. AMATEUR – George T. Dunlap, Kenwood CC (6&5)

Runner(s) Up: Max Marston

BRITISH AMATEUR – Hon. Michael Scott, Royal Liverpool (4&3)

Runner(s) Up: T.A. Bourn

HIGHLIGHTS

- Denny Shute defeats Craig Wood in a 36-hole playoff at St. Andrews.

- Augusta National Golf Club opens for play on January 13th.

1934

LEADING MONEY WINNER – Paul Runyan $6,767

MAJOR WINNERS:
MASTERS – Horton Smith, Augusta National (-4)
Runner(s) Up: Craig Wood (-3)
U.S. OPEN – Olin Dutra, Merion GC (+13)
Runner(s) Up: Gene Sarazen (+14)
THE OPEN – Henry Cotton, Royal St. Georges (+3)
Runner(s) Up: Sid Brews (+8)
PGA CHAMPIONSHIP – Paul Runyan, Park CC (38 holes)
Runner(s) Up: Craig Wood
U.S. AMATEUR CHAMPION – Lawson Little Jr., The Country Club, (8&7)
Runner Up: David Goldman
BRITISH AMATEUR CHAMPION – Lawson Little, Prestwick (14&13)
Runner Up: James Wallace

HIGHLIGHTS
- First ever Masters tournament is held at Augusta National G.C.
- The year that the PGA Tour began naming a Leading Money Winner.
- U.S. and British Amateur tournaments no longer considered majors, being replaced by The Masters and PGA Championship.

1935

LEADING MONEY WINNER – Johnny Revolta $9,543

MAJOR WINNERS:

MASTERS – Gene Sarazen, Augusta National (-6)
Runner(s) Up: Craig Wood (-6)
U.S. OPEN – Sam Parks, Oakmont CC (+11)
Runner(s) Up: Jimmy Thomson (+13)
THE OPEN – Alfred Perry, Muirfield (-5)
Runner(s) Up: Alfred Padgham (-1)
PGA CHAMPIONSHIP – Johnny Revolta, Twin Hills CC (5&4)
Runner(s) Up: Tommy Armour
U.S. AMATEUR CHAMPION – Lawson Little Jr., The Country Club (4&2)
Runner Up: Walter Emery
BRITISH AMATEUR CHAMPION – Lawson Little, Royal Lytham & St. Annes (1 up)
Runner Up: Dr. William Tweddell

HIGHLIGHTS

- Gene Sarazen's double eagle in the last round of The Masters on number 15 is sometimes referred to as the "shot heard round the world." In a way, it put The Masters on the map. This shot put him tied for the lead. The final round ended in a tie, and Sarazen defeated Wood by five strokes in the 36-hole playoff. Donald Ross completes Pinehurst No. 2

1936

LEADING MONEY WINNER – Horton Smith $7,682

MAJOR WINNERS:

MASTERS – Horton Smith, Augusta National (-3)

Runner(s) Up: Harry Cooper (-2)

U.S. OPEN – Tony Manero, Balturol GC (-6)

Runner(s) Up: Harry Cooper (-4)

THE OPEN – Alfred Padgham, Royal Liverpool (-9)

Runner(s) Up: James Adams (-8)

PGA CHAMPIONSHIP – Denny Shute, Pinehurst CC (3&2)

Runner(s) Up: Jimmy Thomson

U.S. AMATEUR CHAMPION – John Fischer, Garden City GC (37 holes)

Runner Up: Jack McLean

BRITISH AMATEUR CHAMPION – Hector Thomson, St. Andrews (2 up)

Runner Up: J. Ferrier

HIGHLIGHTS

- There was controversy around Manero's victory at the U.S. Open. Gene Sarazen requested to be paired with him, as they were close friends, believing he could keep Manero calm in the final round. There were arguments that Sarazen was actually giving advice to Manero, but no wrongdoing was found.

1937

LEADING MONEY WINNER – Harry Cooper $14,138

MAJOR WINNERS:
MASTERS – Byron Nelson, Augusta National (-5)
Runner(s) Up: Ralph Guldahl (-3)
U.S. OPEN – Ralph Guldahl, Oakland Hills (-7)
Runner(s) Up: Sam Snead (-5)
THE OPEN – Henry Cotton, Carnoustie Golf Links (+6)
Runner(s) Up: R.A. Whitcombe (+8)
PGA CHAMPIONSHIP – Denny Shute, Pittsburgh FC (37 holes)
Runner(s) Up: Harold McSpaden
U.S. AMATEUR CHAMPION – John Goodman, Alderwood CC (2 up)
Runner Up: Raymond Billows
BRITISH AMATEUR CHAMPION – Robert Sweeny Jr., Royal
St. George's (3 & 2)
Runner Up: Lionel Munn

HIGHLIGHTS
- Women's inaugural Titleholders Championship at Augusta C.C.

1938

LEADING MONEY WINNER – Sam Snead $19,534

MAJOR WINNERS:

MASTERS – Henry Picard, Augusta National (-3)
Runner(s) Up: Harry Cooper, Ralph Guldahl (-1)
U.S. OPEN – Ralph Guldahl, Cherry Hills CC (E)
Runner(s) Up: Dick Metz (+6)
THE OPEN – R.A. Whitcombe, Royal St. Georges (+15)
Runner(s) Up: James Adams (+17)
PGA CHAMPIONSHIP – Paul Runyan, Shawnee CC (8&7)
Runner(s) Up: Sam Snead
U.S. AMATEUR CHAMPION – William Turnesa, Oakmont CC (8&7)
Runner Up: B. Patrick Abbott
BRITISH AMATEUR CHAMPION – Charlie Yates, Troon (3&2)
Runner Up: Cecil Ewing

HIGHLIGHTS
* USGA implements the 14-club rule.
* First year that the Great Britain amateurs defeated the U.S. in the Walker Cup.

1939

LEADING MONEY WINNER – Henry Picard $10,303

MAJOR WINNERS:

MASTERS – Ralph Guldahl, Augusta National (-9)
Runner(s) Up: Sam Snead (-8)
U.S. OPEN – Byron Nelson, Philadelphia CC (+8)
Runner(s) Up: Craig Wood, Denny Shute (+8)

THE OPEN – Dick Burton, St. Andrews (-2)

Runner(s) Up: Johnny Bulla (E)

PGA CHAMPIONSHIP – Henry Picard, Pomonok CC (37 holes)

Runner(s) Up: Byron Nelson

U.S. AMATEUR CHAMPION – Marvin Ward, North Shore CC (7&5)

Runner Up: Raymond Billows

BRITISH AMATEUR CHAMPION – Alex Kyle, Royal Liverpool (2&1)

Runner Up: Tony Duncan

HIGHLIGHTS

- Byron Nelson defeated both Craig Wood and Denny Shute in U.S. Open. Shute was eliminated after the first 18 holes, while Nelson and Wood tied once again, so they had to play another 18. Nelson beat Wood by three strokes in the second 18.

1940

LEADING MONEY WINNER – Ben Hogan $10,655

MAJOR WINNERS:

MASTERS – Jimmy Demaret, Augusta National (-8)

Runner(s) Up: Lloyd Mangrum (-4)

U.S. OPEN – Lawson Little, Canterbury GC (-1)

Runner(s) Up: Gene Sarazen (-1)

THE OPEN – None due to WWII

PGA CHAMPIONSHIP – Byron Nelson, Hershey CC (1 up)

Runner(s) Up: Sam Snead

U.S. AMATEUR CHAMPION – Richard Chapman, Winged Foot GC (11&9)

Runner Up: W.B. McCullough Jr.

BRITISH AMATEUR CHAMPION – None due to WWII

HIGHLIGHTS

- The U.S. Open ended with an 18-hole playoff.
- British Open and Amateur did not occur due to the Second World War. Golf Courses were converted to airfields and other wartime locations.

1941

LEADING MONEY WINNER – Ben Hogan $18,358

MAJOR WINNERS:

MASTERS – Craig Wood, Augusta National (-8)

Runner(s) Up: Byron Nelson (-5)

U.S. OPEN – Craig Wood, Colonial CC (+4)

Runner(s) Up: Denny Shute (+7)

THE OPEN – None due to WWII

PGA CHAMPIONSHIP – Vic Ghezzi, Cherry Hills CC (38 holes)

Runner(s) Up: Byron Nelson

U.S. AMATEUR CHAMPION – Marvin Ward, Omaha Field Club (4&3)

Runner Up: B. Patrick Abbott

BRITISH AMATEUR CHAMPION – None due to WWII

HIGHLIGHTS

- The U.S. OPEN saw its youngest player to date, Tyrrell Garth. He was a month short of turning 16-years-old. Unfortunately after a first round 80, he withdrew during the second round for unknown reasons. His record age as the youngest stood until 2006 when Tadd Fujikawa broke it.

1942

LEADING MONEY WINNER – Ben Hogan $13,143

MAJOR WINNERS:
MASTERS – Byron Nelson, Augusta National (-8)
Runner(s) Up: Ben Hogan (-8)
U.S. OPEN – None due to WWII
THE OPEN – None due to WWII
PGA CHAMPIONSHIP – Sam Snead, Seaview CC (2&1)
Runner(s) Up: Jim Turnesa
U.S. AMATEUR CHAMPION – None due to WWII
BRITISH AMATEUR CHAMPION – None due to WWII

HIGHLIGHTS
- Byron Nelson beat Ben Hogan by one shot in an 18-hole play-off at The Masters.
- Price of golf balls rises dramatically because of the wartime rubber shortage.

1943

LEADING MONEY WINNER – No stats compiled

MAJOR WINNERS:

MASTERS – None due to WWII

U.S. OPEN – None due to WWII

THE OPEN – None due to WWII

PGA CHAMPIONSHIP – None due to WWII

U.S. AMATEUR CHAMPION – None due to WWII

BRITISH AMATEUR CHAMPION – None due to WWII

HIGHLIGHTS

- No golf majors took place because of WWII

1944

LEADING MONEY WINNER – Byron Nelson $37,967 (war bonds)

MAJOR WINNERS:

MASTERS – None due to WWII

U.S. OPEN – None due to WWII

THE OPEN – None due to WWII

PGA CHAMPIONSHIP – Bob Hamilton, Manito G&CC (1 up)
Runner(s) Up: Byron Nelson

U.S. AMATEUR CHAMPION – None due to WWII

BRITISH AMATEUR CHAMPION – None due to WWII

HIGHLIGHTS

- PGA Tour expands to 22 events, even though many tour players are gone due to military obligations.

1945

LEADING MONEY WINNER – Byron Nelson $63,335 (war bonds)

MAJOR WINNERS:
MASTERS – None due to WWII
U.S. OPEN – None due to WWII
THE OPEN – None due to WWII
PGA CHAMPIONSHIP – Byron Nelson, Moraine CC (4&3)
Runner(s) Up: Sam Byrd
U.S. AMATEUR CHAMPION – None due to WWII
BRITISH AMATEUR CHAMPION – None due to WWII

HIGHLIGHTS
- Byron Nelson won a record 11 straight events on his way to winning 18 in the year (all-time PGA Tour records). He also had a record 19 straight rounds under 70.

1946

LEADING MONEY WINNER – Ben Hogan $42,556

MAJOR WINNERS:
MASTERS – Herman Keiser, Augusta National (-6)

Runner(s) Up: Ben Hogan (-5)

U.S. OPEN – Lloyd Mangrum, Canterbury GC (-4)

Runner(s) Up: Victor Ghezzi, Byron Nelson (-4)

THE OPEN – Sam Snead, St. Andrews (-2)

Runner(s) Up: Johnny Bulla, Bobby Locke (+2)

PGA CHAMPIONSHIP – Ben Hogan, Portland GC (6&4)

Runner(s) Up: Ed Oliver

U.S. AMATEUR CHAMPION – Stanley "Ted" Bishop, Baltusrol GC (37 holes)

Runner Up: Smiley Quick

BRITISH AMATEUR CHAMPION – Jimmy Bruen Jr., Birkdale (4&3)

Runner Up: Robert Sweeny Jr.

HIGHLIGHTS

- It took Lloyd Mangrum two playoffs to win the U.S. Open. All three players tied after the first 18 holes.
- First Women's U.S. Open is held at Spokane CC.

1947

LEADING MONEY WINNER – Jimmy Demaret $27,936

MAJOR WINNERS:

MASTERS – Jimmy Demaret, Augusta National (-7)

Runner(s) Up: Byron Nelson, Frank Stranahan (-5)

U.S. OPEN – Lew Worsham, St. Louis CC (-2)

Runner(s) Up: Sam Snead (-2)

THE OPEN – Fred Daly, Royal Liverpool (+21)

Runner(s) Up: Reggie Horne, Frank Stranahan (+22)

PGA CHAMPIONSHIP – Jim Ferrier, Plum Hollow GC (2&1)
Runner(s) Up: Chick Harbert
U.S. AMATEUR CHAMPION – Robert "Skee" Riegel, Del
Monte Golf & Country Club (2&1)
Runner Up: John Dawson
BRITISH AMATEUR CHAMPION – William Turnesa,
Carnoustie (3&2)
Runner Up: Dick Chapman

HIGHLIGHTS

- The U.S. Open ended in a controversial fashion. Worsham and
  Snead were tied on the 18th green, and Worsham asked an official who was furthest away from the hole, just as Snead was
  about to putt. Snead missed, and Worsham made the putt to
  beat him by one.
- Golf is televised for the first time. The U.S. Open was on a
  local St. Louis TV station.

1948

LEADING MONEY WINNER – Ben Hogan $32,112

MAJOR WINNERS:

MASTERS – Claude Harmon, Augusta National (-9)
Runner(s) Up: Cary Middlecoff (-4)
U.S. OPEN – Ben Hogan, Riviera CC (-8)
Runner(s) Up: Jimmy Demaret (-6)
THE OPEN – Henry Cotton, Muirfield (E)
Runner(s) Up: Fred Daly (+5)

PGA CHAMPIONSHIP – Ben Hogan, Norwood Hills CC (2&1)
Runner(s) Up: Mike Turnesa
U.S. AMATEUR CHAMPION – William P. Turnesa, Memphis CC (2&1)
Runner Up: Raymond Billows
BRITISH AMATEUR CHAMPION – Frank Stranahan, Royal St. George's (5&4)
Runner Up: Charlie Stowe

HIGHLIGHTS

- First U.S. Junior Amateur Championship is held.
- Bobby Locke sets a PGA Tour record for largest winning margin, winning the Chicago Victory National Championship by 16 strokes.

1949

LEADING MONEY WINNER – Sam Snead $31,598

MAJOR WINNERS:

MASTERS – Sam Snead, Augusta National (-6)
Runner(s) Up: Johnny Bulla, Lloyd Mangrum (-3)
U.S. OPEN – Cary Middlecoff, Medinah CC (+2)
Runner(s) Up: Clayton Heafner, Sam Snead (+3)
THE OPEN – Bobby Locke, Royal St. Georges (-5)
Runner(s) Up: Harry Bradshaw (-5)
PGA CHAMPIONSHIP – Sam Snead, Hermitage CC (3&2)
Runner(s) Up: Johnny Palmer
U.S. AMATEUR CHAMPION – Charles Coe, Oak Hill CC (11&10)
Runner Up: Rufus King

BRITISH AMATEUR CHAMPION – Max McCready, Portmarnock (2&1)
Runner Up: William Turnesa

HIGHLIGHTS

- Bobby Locke became the first South African to win THE OPEN, winning in a 36-hole playoff against Bradshaw by 12 strokes.
- First year that The Masters Champion received a green jacket.

1950

LEADING MONEY WINNER – Sam Snead $35,758

MAJOR WINNERS:

MASTERS – Jimmy Demaret, Augusta National (-5)
Runner(s) Up: Jim Ferrier (-3)
U.S. OPEN – Ben Hogan, Merion GC (+7)
Runner(s) Up: George Fazio, Lloyd Mangrum (+7)
THE OPEN – Bobby Locke, Royal Troon (-9)
Runner(s) Up: Roberto De Vicenzo (-7)
PGA CHAMPIONSHIP – Chandler Harper, Scioto CC (4&3)
Runner(s) Up: Henry Williams Jr.
U.S. AMATEUR CHAMPION – Sam Urzetta, Minneapolis GC (39 holes)
Runner Up: Frank Stranahan
BRITISH AMATEUR CHAMPION – Frank Stranahan, St. Andrews (8&6)

Runner Up: Dick Chapman

HIGHLIGHTS

- Ben Hogan won the U.S. Open in an 18-hole playoff against Lloyd Mangrum, only weeks after returning to golf after a near-fatal car accident the year before.
- LPGA is founded to replace the struggling WPGA.

1951

LEADING MONEY WINNER – Lloyd Mangrum $26,068

MAJOR WINNERS:

MASTERS – Ben Hogan, Augusta National (-8)
Runner(s) Up: Skee Riegel (-6)
U.S. OPEN – Ben Hogan, Oakland Hills CC (+7)
Runner(s) Up: Clayton Heafner (+9)
THE OPEN – Max Faulkner, Royal Portrush (-3)
Runner(s) Up: Antonio O. Cerda (-1)
PGA CHAMPIONSHIP – Sam Snead, Oakmont CC (7&6)
Runner(s) Up: Walter Burkemo
U.S. AMATEUR CHAMPION – Billy Maxwell, Saucon Valley CC (4&3)
Runner Up: Joseph F. Gagliardi
BRITISH AMATEUR CHAMPION – Dick Chapman, Royal Porthcawl (5&4)
Runner Up: Charlie Coe

HIGHLIGHTS

- The R&A and the USGA have a conference about the rules of golf. They settled many controversial rules that they had previous conflict over, including legalizing the center-shafted putter and getting rid of the stymie (see "Golf Terms" chapter).

1952

LEADING MONEY WINNER – Julius Boros $37,032

MAJOR WINNERS:

MASTERS – Sam Snead, Augusta National (-2)
Runner(s) Up: Jack Burke Jr. (+2)
U.S. OPEN – Julius Boros, Northwood Club (+1)
Runner(s) Up: Ed Oliver (+5)
THE OPEN – Bobby Locke, Royal Lytham & St. Annes (-1)
Runner(s) Up: Peter Thomson (E)
PGA CHAMPIONSHIP – Jim Turnesa, Big Spring CC (1 up)
Runner(s) Up: Chick Harbert
U.S. AMATEUR CHAMPION – Jack Westland, Seattle GC (3&2)
Runner Up: Al Mengert
BRITISH AMATEUR CHAMPION – Harvie Ward, Prestwick (7&5)
Runner Up: Frank Stranahan

HIGHLIGHTS

- Julius Boros' win at the U.S. OPEN was his first win on the PGA Tour at age 32. This was his breakthrough moment, as he would go on to win 17 more tournaments in his career, including the 1968 PGA Championship where he became the oldest winner at age 48.

1953

LEADING MONEY WINNER – Lew Worsham $34,002

MAJOR WINNERS:
MASTERS – Ben Hogan, Augusta National (-14)
Runner(s) Up: Ed Oliver (-9)
U.S. OPEN – Ben Hogan, Oakmont CC (-5)
Runner(s) Up: Sam Snead (+1)
THE OPEN – Ben Hogan, Carnoustie (-6)
Runner(s) Up: Antonio O. Cerda, Dai Rees, Frank Stranahan, Peter Thomson (-2)
PGA CHAMPIONSHIP – Walter Burkemo, Birmingham CC (2&1)
Runner(s) Up: Felice Torza
U.S. AMATEUR CHAMPION – Gene Littler, Oklahoma City G&CC (1 up)
Runner Up: Dale Morey
BRITISH AMATEUR CHAMPION – Joe Carr, Royal Liverpool (2 up)
Runner Up: Harvie Ward

HIGHLIGHTS
- Ben Hogan completed the first three legs of the modern "Grand Slam," but the OPEN and PGA Championship overlapped, so he never got a chance to complete it with a PGA win.
- First ever golf tournament televised nationwide was the Tam O'Shanter World Championship.

1954

LEADING MONEY WINNER – Bob Toski $65,819

MAJOR WINNERS:

MASTERS – Sam Snead, Augusta National (+1)

Runner(s) Up: Ben Hogan (+1)

U.S. OPEN – Ed Furgol, Baltusrol GC (+4)

Runner(s) Up: Gene Littler (+5)

THE OPEN – Peter Thomson, Royal Birkdale (-9)

Runner(s) Up: Bobby Locke, Dai Rees, Sid Scott (-8)

PGA CHAMPIONSHIP – Chick Harbert, Keller GC (4&3)

Runner(s) Up: Walter Burkemo

U.S. AMATEUR CHAMPION – Arnold Palmer, CC of Detroit (1 up)

Runner Up: Robert Sweeny

BRITISH AMATEUR CHAMPION – D W Bachli, Muirfield (2&1)

Runner Up: Bill Campbell

HIGHLIGHTS

- Snead and Hogan had a dramatic face-off in the 18-hole playoff at The Masters. Snead ended up winning his third and final Masters by one stroke.
- The U.S. Open is televised across the nation (first time).

1955

LEADING MONEY WINNER – Julius Boros $63,121

MAJOR WINNERS:

MASTERS – Cary Middlecoff, Augusta National (-9)

Runner(s) Up: Ben Hogan (-2)

U.S. OPEN – Jack Fleck, Olympic Club (+7)

Runner(s) Up: Ben Hogan (+7)

THE OPEN – Peter Thomson, St. Andrews (-7)

Runner(s) Up: John Fallon (-5)

PGA CHAMPIONSHIP – Doug Ford, Meadowbrook CC (4&3)

Runner(s) Up: Cary Middlecoff

U.S. AMATEUR CHAMPION – E. Harvie Ward Jr., CC of Virginia (9&8)

Runner Up: William Hyndman Jr.

BRITISH AMATEUR CHAMPION – Joe Conrad, Royal Lytham & St. Annes (3&2)

Runner Up: Alan Slater

HIGHLIGHTS

- Fleck's victory over Ben Hogan at the U.S. Open was one of the greatest upsets in all of golf history. Fleck even beat him by three strokes in the 18-hole playoff.

1956

LEADING MONEY WINNER – Ted Kroll $72,835

MAJOR WINNERS:

MASTERS – Jack Burke, Jr., Augusta National (+1)

Runner(s) Up: Ken Venturi (+2)

U.S. OPEN – Cary Middlecoff, Oak Hill CC (+1)

Runner(s) Up: Julius Boros, Ben Hogan (+2)

THE OPEN – Peter Thomson, Royal Liverpool (-2)

Runner(s) Up: Flory Van Donck (+1)

PGA CHAMPIONSHIP – Jack Burke Jr., Blue Hill CC (3&2)

Runner(s) Up: Ted Kroll

U.S. AMATEUR CHAMPION – E. Harvie Ward Jr., Knollwood Club (5&4)

Runner Up: Charles Kocsis

BRITISH AMATEUR CHAMPION – John Beharrell, Troon (5&4)

Runner Up: Leslie G. Taylor

HIGHLIGHTS

- Peter Thomson wins his third OPEN in a row, a feat very few have achieved.

1957

LEADING MONEY WINNER – Dick Mayer $65,835

MAJOR WINNERS:

MASTERS – Doug Ford, Augusta National (-5)

Runner(s) Up: Sam Snead (-2)

U.S. OPEN – Dick Mayer, Inverness Club (+2)

Runner(s) Up: Cary Middlecoff (+2)

THE OPEN – Bobby Locke, St. Andrews (-9)

Runner(s) Up: Peter Thomson (-6)

PGA CHAMPIONSHIP – Lionel Hebert, Miami Valley CC (2&1)

Runner(s) Up: Dow Finsterwald

U.S. AMATEUR CHAMPION – Hillman Robbins Jr., The Country Club (Brookline) (5&4)

Runner Up: Frank M. Taylor

BRITISH AMATEUR CHAMPION – Robert Reid Jack, Formby (2&1)

Runner Up: Harold B. Ridgley

HIGHLIGHTS

- Mayer dominated Middlecoff in the 18-hole U.S. Open playoff. He won by seven strokes.
- Jack Nicklaus played in his first U.S. Open, but missed the cut.

1958

LEADING MONEY WINNER – Arnold Palmer $42,607

MAJOR WINNERS:

MASTERS – Arnold Palmer, Augusta National (-4)

Runner(s) Up: Doug Ford, Fred Hawkins (-3)

U.S. OPEN – Tommy Bolt, Southern Hills CC (+3)

Runner(s) Up: Gary Player (+7)

THE OPEN – Peter Thomson, Royal Lytham & St. Annes (-10)

Runner(s) Up: Dave Thomas (-10)

*PGA CHAMPIONSHIP – Dow Finsterwald, Llanerch CC (-14)

Runner(s) Up: Billy Casper (-12)

U.S. AMATEUR CHAMPION – Charles Coe, The Olympic Club (5&4)
Runner Up: Tommy Aaron
BRITISH AMATEUR CHAMPION – Joe Carr, St. Andrews (3&2)
Runner Up: Alan Thirlwell

HIGHLIGHTS

- Thomson won yet another OPEN, winning a 36-hole playoff by four strokes against Thomas.

  *First year that the PGA Championship was stroke play.

1959

LEADING MONEY WINNER – Art Wall $58,167

MAJOR WINNERS:

MASTERS – Art Wall, Augusta National (-4)
Runner(s) Up: Cary Middlecoff (-3)
U.S. OPEN – Billy Casper, Winged Foot GC (+2)
Runner(s) Up: Bob Rosburg (+3)
THE OPEN – Gary Player, Muirfield (E)
Runner(s) Up: Fred Bullock, Flory Van Donck (+2)
PGA CHAMPIONSHIP – Bob Rosburg, Minneapolis GC (-3)
Runner(s) Up: Jerry Barber, Doug Sanders (-2)
U.S. AMATEUR CHAMPION – Jack Nicklaus, Broadmoor GC (1 up)
Runner Up: Charles Coe
BRITISH AMATEUR CHAMPION – Deane Beman, Royal St. George's (3&2)
Runner Up: Bill Hyndman III

HIGHLIGHTS
The year that *Golf Magazine* began.

1960

LEADING MONEY WINNER – Arnold Palmer $75,262

MAJOR WINNERS:
MASTERS – Arnold Palmer, Augusta National (-6)
Runner(s) Up: Ken Venturi (-5)
U.S. OPEN – Arnold Palmer, Cherry Hills CC (-4)
Runner(s) Up: Jack Nicklaus (-2)
THE OPEN – Kel Nagle, St. Andrews (-10)
Runner(s) Up: Arnold Palmer (-9)
PGA CHAMPIONSHIP – Jay Hebert, Firestone CC (+1)
Runner(s) Up: Jim Ferrier (+2)
U.S. AMATEUR CHAMPION – Deane Beman, St. Louis CC (6&4)
Runner Up: Robert Gardner
BRITISH AMATEUR CHAMPION – Joe Carr, Royal Portrush (8&7)
Runner Up: Bob Cochran

HIGHLIGHTS
- Arnold Palmer's entry into THE OPEN to try and complete the third leg of the current "Grand Slam" brought more American attention to the tournament.
- Players were now allowed to lift, clean, and place balls on the putting surface, as well as fix ball marks on the green.

1961

MAJOR WINNERS:

MASTERS – Gary Player, Augusta National (-8)

Runner(s) Up: Charles Coe, Arnold Palmer (-7)

U.S. OPEN – Gene Littler, Oakland Hills CC (+1)

Runner(s) Up: Bob Goalby, Doug Sanders (+2)

THE OPEN – Arnold Palmer, Royal Birkdale (-4)

Runner(s) Up: Dai Rees (-3)

PGA CHAMPIONSHIP – Jerry Barber, Olympia Fields CC (-3)

Runner(s) Up: Don January (-3)

U.S. AMATEUR CHAMPION – Jack Nicklaus, Pebble Beach (8&6)

Runner Up: H. Dudley Wysong Jr.

BRITISH AMATEUR CHAMPION – Michael Bonallack, Turnberry (6&4)

Runner Up: James Walker

HIGHLIGHTS

- Jerry Barber beat Don January by just one stroke after 18 play-off holes at the PGA Championship. Barber made putts of incredible length on the last three holes just to get into the playoff.
- Gary Player was the first non-American to win The Masters.

1962

LEADING MONEY WINNER – Arnold Palmer $81,448

MAJOR WINNERS:
MASTERS – Arnold Palmer, Augusta National (-8)
Runner(s) Up: Gary Player, Dow Finsterwald (-8)
U.S. OPEN – Jack Nicklaus, Oakmont CC (-1)
Runner(s) Up: Arnold Palmer (-1)
THE OPEN – Arnold Palmer, Royal Troon (-12)
Runner(s) Up: Kel Nagle (-6)
PGA CHAMPIONSHIP – Gary Player, Aronimink GC (-2)
Runner(s) Up: Bob Goalby (-1)
U.S. AMATEUR CHAMPION – Labron Harris Jr., Pinehurst No. 2 (1 up)
Runner Up: Downing Gray
BRITISH AMATEUR CHAMPION – Richard D. Davies, Royal Liverpool (1 up)
Runner Up: John K.D. Povall

HIGHLIGHTS
- Palmer shot a 68 in the three-way, 18-hole playoff at The Masters to edge out Player (71) and Finsterwald (77).
- Jack Nicklaus' win over Palmer in the 18-hole playoff at the U.S. Open was far more impressive than it sounds. Arnold Palmer had the crowd all four days, being so close to where he lived, and Jack Nicklaus had never won a PGA Tour event, let alone a major. He ended up besting Palmer by three strokes.

1963

LEADING MONEY WINNER – Arnold Palmer $128,230

MAJOR WINNERS:

MASTERS – Jack Nicklaus, Augusta National (-2)

Runner(s) Up: Tony Lema (-1)

U.S. OPEN – Julius Boros, The Country Club (+9)

Runner(s) Up: Jacky Cupit, Arnold Palmer (+9)

THE OPEN – Bob Charles, Royal Lytham & St. Annes (-7)

Runner(s) Up: Phil Rodgers (-7)

PGA CHAMPIONSHIP – Jack Nicklaus, Dallas Athletic Club (-5)

Runner(s) Up: Dave Ragan (-3)

U.S. AMATEUR CHAMPION – Deane Beman, Wakonda Club (2&1)

Runner Up: Richard Sikes

BRITISH AMATEUR CHAMPION – Michael Lunt, St. Andrews (2 &1)

Runner Up: John G. Blackwell

HIGHLIGHTS

- Julius Boros won the three-way, 18-hole U.S. Open with a 70, over Cupit's 73, and Palmer's 76.
- Charles beat Rodgers in the 18-hole playoff at THE OPEN by nine strokes to become the first New Zealander and the first lefty to win THE OPEN.
- Arnold Palmer was the first player to win over $100,000 in a single season.

1964

LEADING MONEY WINNER – Jack Nicklaus $113,284

MAJOR WINNERS:

MASTERS – Arnold Palmer, Augusta National (-12)
Runner(s) Up: Dave Marr, Jack Nicklaus (-6)
U.S. OPEN – Ken Venturi, Congressional CC (-2)
Runner(s) Up: Tommy Jacobs (+2)
THE OPEN – Tony Lema, St. Andrews (-9)
Runner(s) Up: Jack Nicklaus (-4)
PGA CHAMPIONSHIP – Bobby Nichols, Columbus CC (-9)
Runner(s) Up: Jack Nicklaus, Arnold Palmer (-6)
U.S. AMATEUR CHAMPION – William Campbell, Canterbury
GC (1 up)
Runner Up: Edgar Tutwiler Jr.
BRITISH AMATEUR CHAMPION – Gordon J. Clark, Ganton
(39 holes)
Runner Up: Michael Lunt

HIGHLIGHTS

- Norman Manley, an ordinary man with an unordinary luck for
  aces (he claims to have made 59), made back to back holes-in-
  one on two par-4s in his club championship at Del Valle in
  California

1965

LEADING MONEY WINNER – Jack Nicklaus $140,752

MAJOR WINNERS:

MASTERS – Jack Nicklaus, Augusta National (-17)

Runner(s) Up: Arnold Palmer, Gary Player (-8)

U.S. OPEN – Gary Player, Bellerive CC (+2)

Runner(s) Up: Kel Nagle (+2)

THE OPEN – Peter Thomson, Royal Birkdale (-7)

Runner(s) Up: Brian Huggett, Christy O'Connor Sr. (-5)

PGA CHAMPIONSHIP – Dave Marr, Laurel Valley CC (-4)

Runner(s) Up: Billy Casper, Jack Nicklaus (-2)

U.S. AMATEUR CHAMPION – Robert Murphy, Southern Hills CC (291)

Runner Up: Robert Dickson (292)

BRITISH AMATEUR CHAMPION – Michael Bonallack, Royal Porthcawl (2&1)

Runner Up: Clive A. Clark

HIGHLIGHTS

- Player beat out Nagle by three strokes in their U.S. Open playoff.
- Gary Player became just the third player (at that time) to have won all four modern majors.
- Qualifying "Q" School originates.
- The U.S. Amateur became stroke play, which lasted until 1972.

1966

LEADING MONEY WINNER – Billy Casper $121,944

MAJOR WINNERS:

MASTERS – Jack Nicklaus, Augusta National (E)

Runner(s) Up: Tommy Jacobs, Gay Brewer (E)

U.S. OPEN – Billy Casper, Olympic Club (-2)

Runner(s) Up: Arnold Palmer (-2)

THE OPEN – Jack Nicklaus, Muirfield (-2)

Runner(s) Up: Doug Sanders, Dave Thomas (-1)

PGA CHAMPIONSHIP – Al Geiberger, Firestone CC (E)

Runner(s) Up: Dudley Wysong (+4)

U.S. AMATEUR CHAMPION – Gary Cowan, Merion GC (285)

Runner Up: Deane Beman (285)

BRITISH AMATEUR CHAMPION – Bobby Cole, Carnoustie (3&2)

Runner Up: Ronnie Shade

HIGHLIGHTS

- Nicklaus' win in the three-way playoff at The Masters made him the first to win back-to-back Masters.
- The year of Arnold Palmer's "collapse" of a six-stroke lead with five holes to play in the U.S. Open, followed by a loss of a two-stroke lead after the first nine of the playoff.
- Jack Nicklaus became the fourth player to win all four of golf's modern majors, just a year after Gary Player did.

1967

LEADING MONEY WINNER – Jack Nicklaus $188,998

MAJOR WINNERS:

MASTERS – Gay Brewer, Augusta National (-8)

Runner(s) Up: Bobby Nichols (-7)

U.S. OPEN – Jack Nicklaus, Baltusrol GC (-5)

Runner(s) Up: Arnold Palmer (-1)

THE OPEN – Roberto De Vicenzo, Royal Liverpool (-10)

Runner(s) Up: Jack Nicklaus (-8)

PGA CHAMPIONSHIP – Don January, Columbine CC (-7)

Runner(s) Up: Don Massengale (-7)

U.S. AMATEUR CHAMPION – Robert Dickson, Broadmoor GC (285)

Runner Up: Vinny Giles (286)

BRITISH AMATEUR CHAMPION – Bob Dickson, Formby (2&1)

Runner Up: Ron Cerrudo

HIGHLIGHTS

- January defeated Massengale by two strokes in the 18-hole PGA Championship playoff.
- Charlie Sifford became the first African-American to win a PGA Tour event.

1968

LEADING MONEY WINNER – Billy Casper $205,168

MAJOR WINNERS:

MASTERS – Bob Goalby, Augusta National (-11)

Runner(s) Up: Roberto De Vicenzo (-10)

U.S. OPEN – Lee Trevino, Oak Hill CC (-5)

Runner(s) Up: Jack Nicklaus (-1)

THE OPEN – Gary Player, Carnoustie (+1)

Runner(s) Up: Bob Charles, Jack Nicklaus (+3)

PGA CHAMPIONSHIP – Julius Boros, Pecan Valley CC (+1)

Runner(s) Up: Bob Charles, Arnold Palmer (+2)

U.S. AMATEUR CHAMPION – Bruce Fleisher, Scioto CC (284)

Runner Up: Vinny Giles (285)

BRITISH AMATEUR CHAMPION – Michael Bonallack, Troon (7&6)

Runner Up: Joe Carr

HIGHLIGHTS

- PGA of America and the PGA Tour split. As a result, Tour players became part of the Association of Professional Golfers.
- In The Masters, though it appears that there was an outright winner, runner-up Robert De Vicenzo tied Bob Goalby, but signed the wrong scorecard. On the 17th hole, he signed for a four but had actually made a three. Once he realized the mistake, it was too late, so he lost by a shot. Since he signed for a score that was worse than his actual score, he was not penalized. If it was the other way around, and he signed for a better score, he would have been disqualified.

1969

LEADING MONEY WINNER – Frank Beard $164,707

MAJOR WINNERS:

MASTERS – George Archer, Augusta National (-7)

Runner(s) Up: Billy Casper, George Knudson, Tom Weiskopf (-6)

U.S. OPEN – Orville Moody, Champions GC (+1)

Runner(s) Up: Deane Beman, Al Geiberger, Bob Rosburg (+2)

THE OPEN – Tony Jacklin, Royal Lytham & St. Anne's (-4)

Runner(s) Up: Bob Charles (-2)

PGA CHAMPIONSHIP – Raymond Floyd, NCR CC (-8)

Runner(s) Up: Gary Player (-7)

U.S. AMATEUR CHAMPION – Steve Melnyk, Oakmont CC (286)

Runner Up: Vinny Giles (291)

BRITISH AMATEUR CHAMPION – Michael Bonallack, Royal Liverpool (3 & 2)

Runner Up: Bill Hyndman III

HIGHLIGHTS

- Harbour Town Golf Links, on Hilton Head Island, opens for play.
- Jack Nicklaus and Tony Jacklin created what they and many others have named, "the greatest act of sportsmanship in history" at the Ryder Cup. Nicklaus was in for par on the final hole of their match, and the match was all square, and so were the two countries. Jacklin had left himself a two-footer, a putt that he would probably never miss, but with added pressure, anything could happen. Lucky for Jacklin, Nicklaus shocked the crowd by conceding this putt, leaving the match and entire Ryder Cup as a tie. Nicklaus gained respect across the globe for his sportsmanship that day as neither country won.

1970

LEADING MONEY WINNER – Lee Trevino $157,037

MAJOR WINNERS:

MASTERS – Billy Casper, Augusta National (-9)

Runner(s) Up: Gene Littler (-9)

U.S. OPEN – Tony Jacklin, Hazeltine National GC (-7)

Runner(s) Up: Dave Hill (E)

THE OPEN – Jack Nicklaus, St. Andrews (-5)

Runner(s) Up: Doug Sanders (-5)

PGA CHAMPIONSHIP – Dave Stockton, Southern Hills CC (-1)

Runner(s) Up: Bob Murphy, Arnold Palmer (+1)

U.S. AMATEUR CHAMPION – Lanny Wadkins, Waverly CC (279)

Runner Up: Tom Kite (280)

BRITISH AMATEUR CHAMPION – Michael Bonallack, Royal
County Down (8&7)

Runner Up: Bill Hyndman III

HIGHLIGHTS

- Casper won The Masters in an 18-hole playoff by winning by five strokes.
- This was the first time that THE OPEN playoff was only 18 holes. Nicklaus held onto his one stroke lead on the last hole to best Doug Sanders.
- Bill Burke shot a 57 at Normandie CC, recording the lowest ever 18-hole score.

1971

LEADING MONEY WINNER – Jack Nicklaus $244,490

MAJOR WINNERS:

MASTERS – Charles Coody, Augusta National (-9)

Runner(s) Up: Johnny Miller, Jack Nicklaus (-7)

U.S. OPEN – Lee Trevino, Merion GC (E)

Runner(s) Up: Jack Nicklaus (E)

THE OPEN – Lee Trevino, Royal Birkdale (-14)

Runner(s) Up: Lu-Liang Huan (-13)

PGA CHAMPIONSHIP – Jack Nicklaus, PGA National (-7)

Runner(s) Up: Billy Casper (-5)

U.S. AMATEUR CHAMPION – Gary Cowan, Wilmington CC (280)

Runner Up: Eddie Pearce (283)

BRITISH AMATEUR CHAMPION – Steve Melnyk, Carnoustie (3&2)

Runner Up: Jim Simons

HIGHLIGHTS

- On the moon, astronaut Alan Shepard hit a 6-iron at the so-called "Fra Mauro Country Club."
- Lee Trevino won the U.S. OPEN and THE OPEN in the same year. The last time this happened was in 1953 when Ben Hogan did it.
- At the U.S. OPEN, Trevino won in an 18-hole playoff by shooting 68 (-2) to Nicklaus' 71 (+1).

1972

LEADING MONEY WINNER – Jack Nicklaus $320,542

MAJOR WINNERS:

MASTERS – Jack Nicklaus, Augusta National (-2)

Runner(s) Up: Bruce Crampton, Bobby Mitchell, Tom Weiskopf (+1)

U.S. OPEN – Jack Nicklaus, Pebble Beach (+2)
Runner(s) Up: Bruce Crampton (+5)
THE OPEN – Lee Trevino, Muirfield (-6)
Runner(s) Up: Jack Nicklaus (-5)
PGA CHAMPIONSHIP – Gary Player, Oakland Hills CC (+1)
Runner(s) Up: Tommy Aaron, Jim Jamieson (+3)
U.S. AMATEUR CHAMPION – Vinny Giles, Charlotte CC (285)
Runner Up: Mark S. Hayes, Ben Crenshaw (288)
BRITISH AMATEUR CHAMPION – T.W.B. Homer, Royal St.
George's (4&3)
Runner Up: Alan Thirlwell

HIGHLIGHTS

- Spalding introduced the first ever two-piece golf ball. They called it a "Top-Flite." Today, nearly every golf ball is made of three pieces.
- Dick Kimbrough, one of the firsts in the speed golf realm, set a record when he played North Plate, Nebraska in 30 minutes and 10 seconds. This was later broken in 1979.

1973

LEADING MONEY WINNER – Jack Nicklaus $308,362

MAJOR WINNERS:

MASTERS – Tommy Aaron, Augusta National (-5)
Runner(s) Up: J.C. Snead (-4)
U.S. OPEN – Johnny Miller, Oakmont CC (-5)
Runner(s) Up: John Schlee (-4)

THE OPEN – Tom Weiskopf, Royal Troon (-12)

Runner(s) Up: Neil Coles, Johnny Miller (-9)

PGA CHAMPIONSHIP – Jack Nicklaus, Canterbury GC (-7)

Runner(s) Up: Bruce Crampton (-3)

U.S. AMATEUR CHAMPION – Craig Stadler, Inverness Club (6&5)

Runner Up: David Strawn

BRITISH AMATEUR CHAMPION – Dick Siderowf, Royal Porthcawl (5&3)

Runner Up: P.H. Moody

HIGHLIGHTS

- First year of an all-match play U.S. Amateur Championship
- Ben Crenshaw won the NCAA men's golf title for his third year in a row. He then proceeded to earn his Tour card and win the first event he played in, the San Antonio-Texas Open.
- Nicklaus' win at the PGA Championship broke Bobby Jones' record of most major victories. Nicklaus now had 14 and proceeded to break his own record several times.

1974

LEADING MONEY WINNER – Johnny Miller $353,021

MAJOR WINNERS:

MASTERS – Gary Player, Augusta National (-10)

Runner(s) Up: Dave Stockton, Tom Weiskopf (-8)

U.S. OPEN – Hale Irwin, Winged Foot GC (+7)

Runner(s) Up: Forrest Fezler (+9)

THE OPEN – Gary Player, Royal Lytham & St. Annes (-2)

Runner(s) Up: Peter Oosterhuis (+2)

PGA CHAMPIONSHIP – Lee Trevino, Tanglewood GC (-4)

Runner(s) Up: Jack Nicklaus (-3)

THE PLAYERS – Jack Nicklaus, Atlanta CC (-16)

Runner(s) Up: J.C. Snead (-14)

U.S. AMATEUR CHAMPION – Jerry Pate, Ridgewood CC
(2&1)

Runner Up: John P. Grace

BRITISH AMATEUR CHAMPION – T.W.B. Homer, Muirfield
(2 up)

Runner Up: Jimmy Gabrielsen

HIGHLIGHTS

- First year of The Players championship.
- World Golf Hall of Fame opened in Pinehurst, North Carolina.
- A golfer by the name of Mike Austin hit a 516-yard drive at the National Seniors Open. This is the longest drive recorded in a competition.

1975

LEADING MONEY WINNER – Jack Nicklaus $298,149

MAJOR WINNERS:

MASTERS – Jack Nicklaus, Augusta National (-12)

Runner(s) Up: Johnny Miller, Tom Weiskopf (-11)

U.S. OPEN – Lou Graham, Medinah CC (+3)

Runner(s) Up: John Mahaffey (+3)

THE OPEN – Tom Watson, Carnoustie (-9)

Runner(s) Up: Jack Newton (-9)

PGA CHAMPIONSHIP – Jack Nicklaus, Firestone CC (-4)

Runner(s) Up: Bruce Crampton (-2)

THE PLAYERS – Al Geiberger, Colonial CC (-10)

Runner(s) Up: Dave Stockton (-7)

U.S. AMATEUR CHAMPION – Fred Ridley, CC of Virginia (2 up)

Runner Up: Keith Fergus

BRITISH AMATEUR CHAMPION – Vinny Giles III, Royal Liverpool (8&7)

Runner Up: Mark James

HIGHLIGHTS

- Both OPENs ended in playoffs and were headlined for the collapses of their overnight leaders.
- In the U.S. OPEN, Frank Beard held a 3-stroke lead going into Sunday and shot a final round 78 (+7) to land him only one shot off. In the playoff, Lou Graham shot a 71 (E) to Mahaffey's 73 (+2).
- At THE OPEN, Bobby Cole had just a 1-stroke advantage, and finished a stroke out of the playoff with a 76 (+4) in the final round. Tom Watson's 71 (-1) beat Jack Newton's 72 (E).

1976

LEADING MONEY WINNER – Jack Nicklaus $266,498

MAJOR WINNERS:

MASTERS – Raymond Floyd, Augusta National (-17)

Runner(s) Up: Ben Crenshaw (-9)

U.S. OPEN – Jerry Pate, Atlanta Athletic Club (-3)

Runner(s) Up: Al Geiberger, Tom Weiskopf (-1)

THE OPEN – Johnny Miller, Royal Birkdale (-9)

Runner(s) Up: Seve Ballesteros, Jack Nicklaus (-3)

PGA CHAMPIONSHIP – Dave Stockton, Congressional CC (+1)

Runner(s) Up: Raymond Floyd, Don January (+2)

THE PLAYERS – Jack Nicklaus, Inverrary CC (-19)

Runner(s) Up: J.C. Snead (-16)

U.S. AMATEUR CHAMPION – Bill Sander, Bel-Air CC (8&6)

Runner Up: C. Parker Moore Jr.

BRITISH AMATEUR CHAMPION – Dick Siderowf, St. Andrews (37 holes)

Runner Up: John C. Davies

HIGHLIGHTS

- Jerry Pate, a rookie, stuck a gutsy shot over the water to two feet in the final round of the U.S. OPEN, right after his playing partner hit the same shot in the water. Pate would go on to win.
- USGA implemented an Overall Distance Standard, banning golf balls that flew more than 280 yards on of their standard tests.

1977

LEADING MONEY WINNER – Tom Watson $310,653

MAJOR WINNERS:

MASTERS – Tom Watson, Augusta National (-12)

Runner(s) Up: Jack Nicklaus (-10)

U.S. OPEN – Hubert Green, Southern Hills CC (-2)

Runner(s) Up: Lou Graham (-1)

THE OPEN – Tom Watson, Turnberry (-12)

Runner(s) Up: Jack Nicklaus (-11)

PGA CHAMPIONSHIP – Lanny Wadkins, Pebble Beach (-6)

Runner(s) Up: Gene Littler (-6)

THE PLAYERS – Mark Hayes, Sawgrass CC (+1)

Runner(s) Up: Mike McCullough (+3)

U.S. AMATEUR CHAMPION – John Fought, Aronimink GC (9&8)

Runner Up: Doug Fischesser

BRITISH AMATEUR CHAMPION – Peter McEvoy, Ganton (5&4)

Runner Up: Hugh M. Campbell

HIGHLIGHTS

- Al Geiberger set a PGA Tour record of lowest round of 18 with a 59 at Colonial CC.
- At the PGA Championship, the first "sudden death" playoff occurred in a major. It took three holes to settle it, but Wadkins came out on top, getting up and down for par as Littler failed to do the same.

1978

LEADING MONEY WINNER – Tom Watson $362,428

MAJOR WINNERS:

MASTERS – Gary Player, Augusta National (-11)

Runner(s) Up: Rod Funseth, Hubert Green, Tom Watson (-10)

U.S. OPEN – Andy North, Cherry Hills CC (+1)

Runner(s) Up: J.C. Snead, Dave Stockton (+2)

THE OPEN – Jack Nicklaus, St. Andrews (-7)

Runner(s) Up: Ben Crenshaw, Raymond Floyd, Tom Kite, Simon Owen (-5)

PGA CHAMPIONSHIP – John Mahaffey, Oakmont CC (-8)

Runner(s) Up: Jerry Pate, Tom Watson (-8)

THE PLAYERS – Jack Nicklaus, Sawgrass CC (+1)

Runner(s) Up: Lou Graham (+2)

U.S. AMATEUR CHAMPION – John Cook, Plainfield CC (5&4)

Runner Up: Scott Hoch

BRITISH AMATEUR CHAMPION – Peter McEvoy, Royal Troon (4&3)

Runner Up: Paul McKellar

HIGHLIGHTS

- Legends of Golf tournament started in Austin, Texas. It was a senior event that would eventually lead to the Senior PGA Tour.
- At the PGA Championship, Tom Watson lost a five-shot lead to fall into a sudden death playoff. All three men parred the first hole, but only Mahaffey was able to birdie the second to win.
- Jack Nicklaus continues his success with a 15th major win at THE OPEN.

1979

LEADING MONEY WINNER – Tom Watson $462,636

MAJOR WINNERS:

MASTERS – Fuzzy Zoeller, Augusta National (-8)

Runner(s) Up: Ed Sneed, Tom Watson (-8)

U.S. OPEN – Hale Irwin, Inverness Club (E)

Runner(s) Up: Jerry Pate, Gary Player (+2)

THE OPEN – Seve Ballesteros, Royal Lytham & St. Annes (-1)

Runner(s) Up: Ben Crenshaw, Jack Nicklaus (+2)

PGA CHAMPIONSHIP – David Graham, Oakland Hills CC (-8)

Runner(s) Up: Ben Crenshaw (-8)

THE PLAYERS – Lanny Wadkins, Sawgrass CC (-5)

Runner(s) Up: Tom Watson (E)

U.S. AMATEUR CHAMPION – Mark O'Meara, Canterbury GC (8&7)

Runner Up: John Cook

BRITISH AMATEUR CHAMPION – Jay Sigel, Hillside (3&2)

Runner Up: Scott Hoch

HIGHLIGHTS

- The Ryder Cup would allow players from the European continent to compete on the side of Europe (not limited to just Irish and British anymore).
- At The Masters, Ed Sneed bogeyed his last three holes, giving up his three-shot lead to fall into a playoff that was won by Fuzzy Zoeller on the second sudden death playoff hole.
- David Graham's playoff victory at the PGA was due to his putting, one-putting all three playoff holes.

1980

LEADING MONEY WINNER – Tom Watson $530,808

MAJOR WINNERS:

MASTERS – Seve Ballesteros, Augusta National (-13)

Runner(s) Up: Gibby Gibbert, Jack Newton (-9)

U.S. OPEN – Jack Nicklaus, Baltusrol (-8)

Runner(s) Up: Isao Aoki (-6)

THE OPEN – Tom Watson, Muirfield (-13)

Runner(s) Up: Lee Trevino (-9)

PGA CHAMPIONSHIP – Jack Nicklaus, Oak Hill CC (-6)

Runner(s) Up: Andy Bean (+1)

THE PLAYERS – Lee Trevino, Sawgrass CC (-10)

Runner(s) Up: Ben Crenshaw (-9)

U.S. AMATEUR CHAMPION – Hal Sutton, CC of North Carolina (9&8)

Runner Up: Bob Lewis

BRITISH AMATEUR CHAMPION – Duncan Evans, Royal Porthcawl (4&3)

Runner Up: David Suddards

HIGHLIGHTS

- The Senior PGA Tour was born and had four official events.
- Jack Nicklaus shot a 72-hole total of 272 at the U.S. OPEN, a record low at that event which was only tied a few times, until Rory McIlroy broke it in 2011 with a 268. Nicklaus also broke his record two more times this year, winning his 16th and 17th majors.
- USGA set a Symmetry Standard that outlawed self-correcting golf balls.

1981

LEADING MONEY WINNER – Tom Kite $375,699

MAJOR WINNERS:

MASTERS – Tom Watson, Augusta National (-8)

Runner(s) Up: Johnny Miller, Jack Nicklaus (-6)

U.S. OPEN – David Graham, Merion (-7)

Runner(s) Up: George Burns, Bill Rogers (-4)

THE OPEN – Bill Rogers, Royal St. Georges (-4)

Runner(s) Up: Bernhard Langer (E)

PGA CHAMPIONSHIP – Larry Nelson, Atlanta Athl. Club (-7)

Runner(s) Up: Fuzzy Zoeller (-3)

THE PLAYERS – Raymond Floyd, Sawgrass CC (-3)

Runner(s) Up: Barry Jaeckel, Curtis Strange (-3)

U.S. AMATEUR CHAMPION – Nathaniel Crosby, The Olympic Club (37 holes)

Runner Up: Brian Lindley

BRITISH AMATEUR CHAMPION – Philippe Ploujoux, St. Andrews (4&2)

Runner Up: Joel Hirsch

HIGHLIGHTS

- TPC Sawgrass opened this year and later became the home of The Players Championship. This course served as a model for the several stadium courses that were built after it.
- US Mid-Am event is added to USGA Championships. This event was for males over the age of 25.
- The Sun City Million Dollar Challenge in South Africa is the first $1 million event, but not on the PGA Tour.

1982

LEADING MONEY WINNER – Craig Stadler $446,462

MAJOR WINNERS:

MASTERS – Craig Stadler, Augusta National (-4)
Runner(s) Up: Dan Pohl (-4)
U.S. OPEN – Tom Watson, Pebble Beach (-6)
Runner(s) Up: Jack Nicklaus (-4)
THE OPEN – Tom Watson, Royal Troon (-4)
Runner(s) Up: Peter Oosterhuis, Nick Price (-3)
PGA CHAMPIONSHIP – Raymond Floyd, Southern Hills CC (-8)
Runner(s) Up: Lanny Wadkins (-5)
THE PLAYERS – Jerry Pate, TPC Sawgrass (-8)
Runner(s) Up: Brad Bryant, Scott Simpson (-6)
U.S. AMATEUR CHAMPION – Jay Sigel, The Country Club
(Brookline) (8&7)
Runner Up: David Tolley
BRITISH AMATEUR CHAMPION – Martin S. Thompson,
Royal Cinque Ports (4&3)
Runner Up: A.K. Stubbs

HIGHLIGHTS

- Tom Watson hit one of the most famous shots in U.S. OPEN
  history. It was a very tricky downhill chip from rough behind the
  17th green. It seemed to many to be almost impossible to get near
  the hole, but Watson holed it for birdie, and carried his momen-
  tum to the 18th hole to finish birdie-birdie. Watson also won his

fourth OPEN with the final round collapse of Bobby Clampett.

- Craig Stadler won The Masters with a par on the first sudden death hole (#10) against Dan Pohl.

1983

LEADING MONEY WINNER – Hal Sutton $426,668

MAJOR WINNERS:

MASTERS – Seve Ballesteros, Augusta National (-8)
Runner(s) Up: Ben Crenshaw, Tom Kite (-4)
U.S. OPEN – Larry Nelson, Oakmont (-4)
Runner(s) Up: Tom Watson (-3)
THE OPEN – Tom Watson, Royal Birkdale (-9)
Runner(s) Up: Andy Bean, Hale Irwin (-8)
PGA CHAMPIONSHIP – Hal Sutton, Riviera CC (-10)
Runner(s) Up: Jack Nicklaus (-9)
THE PLAYERS – Hal Sutton, TPC Sawgrass (-5)
Runner(s) Up: Bob Eastwood (-4)
U.S. AMATEUR CHAMPION – Jay Sigel, North Shore CC (8&7)
Runner Up: Chris Perry
BRITISH AMATEUR CHAMPION – Philip Parkin, Turnberry (5&4)
Runner Up: Jim Holtgrieve

HIGHLIGHTS

- The year that the PGA Tour expanded the "all-exempt" Tour from the top 60 to 125 players from the past year being exempt from weekly qualifying.
- Record 34 unique winners this year.

- THE OPEN was a tight battle with nine holes to play. Seven players were within a single shot of the lead at that point, but Tom Watson came out on top, winning his fifth OPEN.

1984

LEADING MONEY WINNER – Tom Watson $476,260

MAJOR WINNERS:
MASTERS – Ben Crenshaw, Augusta National (-11)
Runner(s) Up: Tom Watson (-9)
U.S. OPEN – Fuzzy Zoeller, Winged Foot (-4)
Runner(s) Up: Greg Norman (-4)
THE OPEN – Seve Ballesteros, St. Andrews (-12)
Runner(s) Up: Bernhard Langer, Tom Watson, (-10)
PGA CHAMPIONSHIP – Lee Trevino, Shoal Creek CC (-15)
Runner(s) Up: Gary Player, Lanny Wadkins (-11)
THE PLAYERS – Fred Couples, TPC Sawgrass (-11)
Runner(s) Up: Lee Trevino (-10)
U.S. AMATEUR CHAMPION – Scott Verplank, Oak Tree GC (4&3)
Runner Up: Sam Randolph
BRITISH AMATEUR CHAMPION – Jose MariaOlazabal, Formby (5&4)
Runner Up: Colin Montgomerie

HIGHLIGHTS
- Jack Nicklaus' Desert Highlands course opens in Phoenix. This is the first "target golf" style course that used only 80 acres of land rather than the typical 100-150 acres. It promoted an era

of more environmentally sensitive desert course designs.

- The U.S. OPEN playoff did not seem to be much of a contest, as Fuzzy Zoeller dominated with a 67 (-3) versus Greg Norman's 75 (+5).

1985

LEADING MONEY WINNER – Curtis Strange $542,321

MAJOR WINNERS:

MASTERS – Bernhard Langer, Augusta National (-6)
Runner(s) Up: Seve Ballesteros, Raymond Floyd, Curtis Strange (-4)
U.S. OPEN – Andy North, Oakland Hills (-1)
Runner(s) Up: Dave Barr, T.C. Chen, Denis Watson (E)
THE OPEN – Sandy Lyle, Royal St. Georges (+2)
Runner(s) Up: Payne Stewart (+3)
PGA CHAMPIONSHIP – Hubert Green, Cherry Hills (-6)
Runner(s) Up: Lee Trevino (-4)
THE PLAYERS – Calvin Peete, TPC Sawgrass (-14)
Runner(s) Up: D.A. Weibring (-11)
U.S. AMATEUR CHAMPION – Sam Randolph, Montclair GC (1 up)
Runner Up: Peter Persons
BRITISH AMATEUR CHAMPION – Garth McGimpsey, Royal Dornoch & Golspie (8&7)
Runner Up: Graham Homewood

HIGHLIGHTS

- Bernhard Langer became the first German to win a major when he won The Masters.

- Europe won the Ryder Cup for the first time since 1957.
- USGA introduced the Slope System to adjust handicaps, which allowed players of different calibers to play on an even playing field.

1986

LEADING MONEY WINNER – Greg Norman $653,296

MAJOR WINNERS:

MASTERS – Jack Nicklaus, Augusta National (-9)

Runner(s) Up: Tom Kite, Greg Norman (-8)

U.S. OPEN – Raymond Floyd, Shinnecock Hills (-1)

Runner(s) Up: Chip Beck, Lanny Wadkins (+1)

THE OPEN – Greg Norman, Turnberry (E)

Runner(s) Up: Gordon J. Brand (+5)

PGA CHAMPIONSHIP – Bob Tway, Inverness (-8)

Runner(s) Up: Greg Norman (-6)

THE PLAYERS – John Mahaffey, TPC Sawgrass (-13)

Runner(s) Up: Larry Mize (-12)

U.S. AMATEUR CHAMPION – Buddy Alexander, Shoal Creek (5&3)

Runner Up: Chris Kite

BRITISH AMATEUR CHAMPION – David Curry, Royal Lytham & St. Annes (11&9)

Runner Up: S. Geoffrey Birtwell

HIGHLIGHTS

- Year of the "Norman Slam:" Greg Norman held/co-held the

54-hole lead for all four championships, but was only able to win one, THE OPEN. It was his first of two Major wins.

- At The Masters, 46-year-old Jack Nicklaus blew past his younger competition with a 65 in the final round. This was his 18th and final major win.
- Las Vegas Invitational was the first PGA Tour event to have a $1 million purse.

1987

LEADING MONEY WINNER – Curtis Strange $925,941

MAJOR WINNERS:

MASTERS – Larry Mize, Augusta National (-3)
Runner(s) Up: Seve Ballesteros, Greg Norman (-3)
U.S. OPEN – Scott Simpson, Olympic Club (-3)
Runner(s) Up: Tom Watson (-2)
THE OPEN – Nick Faldo, Muirfield (-5)
Runner(s) Up: Paul Azinger, Rodger Davis (-4)
PGA CHAMPIONSHIP – Larry Nelson, PGA National (-1)
Runner(s) Up: Lanny Wadkins (-1)
THE PLAYERS – Sandy Lyle, TPC Sawgrass (-14)
Runner(s) Up: Jeff Sluman (-14)
U.S. AMATEUR CHAMPION – Billy Mayfair, Jupiter Hills Club (4&3)
Runner Up: Eric Rebmann
BRITISH AMATEUR CHAMPION – Paul Mayo, Prestwick (3&1)
Runner Up: Peter McEvoy

HIGHLIGHTS

- The Masters had a very surprising ending in the sudden death playoff. After Ballesteros failed to par the first playoff hole, Larry Mize chipped in on the second for an unexpected birdie to edge Greg Norman.
- Nelson got up-and-down on the first playoff hole at the PGA Championship to beat Watkins, who failed to make his four-foot par putt.
- Nick Faldo made 18 straight pars in his final round of THE OPEN to win his first major.

1988

LEADING MONEY WINNER – Curtis Strange $1,147,644

MAJOR WINNERS:

MASTERS – Sandy Lyle, Augusta National (-7)
Runner(s) Up: Mark Calcavecchia (-6)
U.S. OPEN – Curtis Strange, The Country Club (Brookline) (-6)
Runner(s) Up: Nick Faldo (-6)
THE OPEN – Seve Ballesteros, Royal Lytham & St. Annes (-11)
Runner(s) Up: Nick Price (-9)
PGA CHAMPIONSHIP – Jeff Sluman, Oak Tree Golf Club (-12)
Runner(s) Up: Paul Azinger (-9)
THE PLAYERS – Mark McCumber, TPC Sawgrass (-15)
Runner(s) Up: Mike Reid (-11)
U.S. AMATEUR CHAMPION – Eric Meeks, Virginia Hot Springs G&CC (7&6)
Runner Up: Danny Yates

BRITISH AMATEUR CHAMPION – Christian Hardin, Royal Porthcawl (1 up)
Runner Up: Ben Fouchee

HIGHLIGHTS

- Curtis Strange shot a 71 (E) in his 18-hole playoff against Nick Faldo's 75 (+4) to win the U.S. OPEN. This year, Strange also became the first player to win more than $1 million in a season.
- Sandy Lyle was the first British golfer to win The Masters.
- THE OPEN finished on a Monday for the first time ever due to weather delays.

1989

LEADING MONEY WINNER – Tom Kite $1,395,278

MAJOR WINNERS:

MASTERS – Nick Faldo, Augusta National (-5)
Runner(s) Up: Scott Hoch (-5)
U.S. OPEN – Curtis Strange, Oak Hill (-2)
Runner(s) Up: Chip Beck, Mark McCumber, Ian Woosnam (-1)
THE OPEN – Mark Calcavecchia, Royal Troon (-13)
Runner(s) Up: Wayne Grady, Greg Norman (-13)
PGA CHAMPIONSHIP – Payne Stewart, Kemper Lakes (-12)
Runner(s) Up: Andy Bean, Mike Reid, Curtis Strange (-11)
THE PLAYERS – Tom Kite, TPC Sawgrass (-9)
Runner(s) Up: Chip Beck (-8)
U.S. AMATEUR CHAMPION – Chris Patton, Merion GC (3&1)
Runner Up: Danny Green

BRITISH AMATEUR CHAMPION – Stephen Dodd, Royal Birkdale (5&3)
Runner Up: Craig Cassells

HIGHLIGHTS

- Nick Faldo holed a 100-foot putt on the second hole at Augusta National, the longest in a major. Later in a playoff, Scott Hoch missed a two-foot putt on the first playoff hole to lose The Masters to none other than Nick Faldo.
- At THE OPEN, they began using a new 4-hole playoff format. The three players played numbers 1, 2, 17, and 18. Calcavecchia came out on top, finishing at -2 for the four holes.
- At the U.S. OPEN, four players aced the same hole (#6) on the same day at Oak Hill CC.

1990

PLAYER OF THE YEAR – Wayne Levi
LEADING MONEY WINNER – Greg Norman $1,165,477

MAJOR WINNERS:

MASTERS – Nick Faldo, Augusta National (-10)
Runner(s) Up: Raymond Floyd (-10)
U.S. OPEN – Hale Irwin, Medinah (-8)
Runner(s) Up: Mike Donald (-8)
THE OPEN – Nick Faldo, St. Andrews (-18)
Runner(s) Up: Mark McNulty, Payne Stewart (-13)
PGA CHAMPIONSHIP – Wayne Grady, Shoal Creek (-6)

Runner(s) Up: Fred Couples (-3)

THE PLAYERS – Jodie Mudd, TPC Sawgrass (-10)

Runner(s) Up: Mark Calcavecchia (-9)

ROOKIE OF THE YEAR – Robert Gamez

U.S. AMATEUR CHAMPION – Phil Mickelson, Cherry Hills
CC (5&4)

Runner Up: Manny Zerman

BRITISH AMATEUR CHAMPION – Rolf Muntz, Muirfield
(7&6)

Runner Up: Michael Macara

HIGHLIGHTS

- First year with a Player and Rookie of the Year recognized.
- The U.S. OPEN required sudden death holes after the 18-hole playoff for the first time ever. It only took one extra hole, as Hale Irwin birdied it and Donald did not.
- At The Masters, Nick Faldo took down Raymond Floyd after two playoff holes.

1991

PLAYER OF THE YEAR – Fred Couples

LEADING MONEY WINNER – Corey Pavin $979,430

MAJOR WINNERS:

MASTERS – Ian Woosnam, Augusta National (-11)

Runner(s) Up: Jose Maria Olazabal (-10)

U.S. OPEN – Payne Stewart, Hazeltine (-6)

Runner(s) Up: Scott Simpson (-6)

THE OPEN – Ian Baker-Finch, Royal Birkdale (-8)

Runner(s) Up: Mike Harwood (-6)

PGA CHAMPIONSHIP – John Daly, Crooked Stick (-12)

Runner(s) Up: Bruce Lietzke (-9)

THE PLAYERS – Steve Elkington, TPC Sawgrass (-12)

Runner(s) Up: Fuzzy Zoeller (-11)

ROOKIE OF THE YEAR – John Daly

U.S. AMATEUR CHAMPION – Mitch Voges, The Honors Course (7&6)

Runner Up: Manny Zerman

BRITISH AMATEUR CHAMPION – Gary Wolstenholme, Ganton (8&6)

Runner Up: Bob May

HIGHLIGHTS

- Scott Simpson led the 18-hole playoff against Payne Stewart with three holes to play, but lost his two-stroke lead over the last few holes. Stewart won by two with a 75 (+3) to Simpson's 77 (+5).
- John Daly won the PGA Championship after getting into the tournament as a ninth alternate. He found out he got in the night before competition started.

1992

PLAYER OF THE YEAR – Fred Couples

LEADING MONEY WINNER – Fred Couples $1,344,188

MAJOR WINNERS:

MASTERS – Fred Couples, Augusta National (-13)

Runner(s) Up: Raymond Floyd (-11)

U.S. OPEN – Tom Kite, Pebble Beach (-3)

Runner(s) Up: Jeff Sluman (-1)

THE OPEN – Nick Faldo, Muirfield (-12)

Runner(s) Up: John Cook (-11)

PGA CHAMPIONSHIP – Nick Price, Bellerive Country Club (-6)

Runner(s) Up: John Cook, Nick Faldo, Jim Gallagher Jr., Gene Sauers (-3)

THE PLAYERS – Davis Love III, TPC Sawgrass (-15)

Runner(s) Up: Ian Baker-Finch, Phil Blackmar, Nick Faldo, Tom Watson (-11)

ROOKIE OF THE YEAR – Mark Carnevale

U.S. AMATEUR CHAMPION – Justin Leonard, Muirfield Village GC (8&7)

Runner Up: Tom Scherrer

BRITISH AMATEUR CHAMPION – Stephen Dundas, Carnoustie (7&6)

Runner Up: Bradley Dredge

HIGHLIGHTS

- All three majors that take place in the U.S. are won by first-time major winners. Up until this point, they had been successful, but were only runners-up in majors. This was their breakthrough year.
- Two men by the names of Simon Clough and Boris Janic played five rounds of 18 holes in one day. Each round took place in a different country, and they walked each course.

1993

PLAYER OF THE YEAR – Nick Price
LEADING MONEY WINNER – Nick Price $1,478,557

MAJOR WINNERS:

MASTERS – Bernhard Langer, Augusta National (-11)
Runner(s) Up: Chip Beck (-7)
U.S. OPEN – Lee Janzen, Baltusrol (-8)
Runner(s) Up: Payne Stewart (-6)
THE OPEN – Greg Norman, Royal St. Georges (-13)
Runner(s) Up: Nick Faldo (-11)
PGA CHAMPIONSHIP – Paul Azinger, Inverness (-12)
Runner(s) Up: Greg Norman (-12)
THE PLAYERS – Nick Price, TPC Sawgrass (-18)
Runner(s) Up: Bernhard Langer (-13)
ROOKIE OF THE YEAR – Vijay Singh
U.S. AMATEUR CHAMPION – John Harris, Champions GC (5&3)
Runner Up: Danny Ellis
BRITISH AMATEUR CHAMPION – Iain Pyman, Royal Portrush (37 holes)
Runner Up: Paul Page

HIGHLIGHTS

- The PGA Championship took two playoff holes to reach a conclusion. Number 18 served as the first, where Norman and Azinger both barely missed birdies, then number ten was the deciding factor, where Norman three-putted for bogey as Azinger easily tapped in his par putt.
- Plans for The Golf Channel were announced, a 24/7 cable show for golf.

1994

PLAYER OF THE YEAR – Nick Price
LEADING MONEY WINNER – Nick Price $1,499,927

MAJOR WINNERS:

MASTERS – Jose Maria Olazabal, Augusta National (-9)
Runner(s) Up: Tom Lehman (-7)
U.S. OPEN – Ernie Els, Oakmont (-5)
Runner(s) Up: Colin Montgomerie, Loren Roberts (-5)
THE OPEN – Nick Price, Turnberry (-12)
Runner(s) Up: Jesper Parnevik (-11)
PGA CHAMPIONSHIP – Nick Price, Southern Hills (-11)
Runner(s) Up: Corey Pavin (-5)
THE PLAYERS – Greg Norman, TPC Sawgrass (-24)
Runner(s) Up: Fuzzy Zoeller (-20)
ROOKIE OF THE YEAR – Ernie Els
U.S. AMATEUR CHAMPION – Tiger Woods, TPC Sawgrass (2 up)
Runner Up: Trip Kuehne
BRITISH AMATEUR CHAMPION – Lee James, Nairn (2&1)
Runner Up: Gordon Sherry

HIGHLIGHTS

- Ernie Els and Loren Roberts were still tied after the Monday 18-hole playoff at the U.S. OPEN, with 74 (+3), so it went to sudden death holes. They played 10 and 11, where Els managed a par on 11 while Roberts bogeyed.
- Tiger Woods became the youngest winner of the U.S. Amateur at age 18.

1995

PLAYER OF THE YEAR – Greg Norman
LEADING MONEY WINNER – Greg Norman $1,654,959

MAJOR WINNERS:

MASTERS – Ben Crenshaw, Augusta National (-14)
Runner(s) Up: Davis Love III (-13)
U.S. OPEN – Corey Pavin, Shinnecock Hills (E)
Runner(s) Up: Greg Norman (+2)
THE OPEN – John Daly, St. Andrews (-6)
Runner(s) Up: Constantino Rocca (-6)
PGA CHAMPIONSHIP – Steve Elkington, Riviera (-17)
Runner(s) Up: Colin Montgomerie (-17)
THE PLAYERS – Lee Janzen, TPC Sawgrass (-5)
Runner(s) Up: Bernhard Langer (-4)
ROOKIE OF THE YEAR – Woody Austin
U.S. AMATEUR CHAMPION – Tiger Woods, Newport CC (2 up)
Runner Up: Buddy Marucci
BRITISH AMATEUR CHAMPION – Gordon Sherry, Royal Liverpool (7&6)
Runner Up: Michael Reynard

HIGHLIGHTS

- At THE OPEN, a 4-hole playoff took place. On 17 at St. Andrews, Rocca found the Road Bunker, then took three shots to get out. Rocca's finished at +3 for the four holes to Daly's -1.
- The PGA Championship only took one hole to decide a winner. Elkington drained a 20-foot birdie putt on number 18,

and Montgomerie missed his birdie chance from slightly inside that.

1996

PLAYER OF THE YEAR – Tom Lehman
LEADING MONEY WINNER – Tom Lehman $1,780,159

MAJOR WINNERS:

MASTERS – Nick Faldo, Augusta National (-12)
Runner(s) Up: Greg Norman (-7)
U.S. OPEN – Steve Jones, Oakland Hills (-2)
Runner(s) Up: Tom Lehman, Davis Love III (-1)
THE OPEN – Tom Lehman, Royal Lytham & St. Annes (-13)
Runner(s) Up: Ernie Els, Mark McCumber (-11)
PGA CHAMPIONSHIP – Mark Brooks, Valhalla (-11)
Runner(s) Up: Kenny Perry (-11)
THE PLAYERS – Fred Couples, TPC Sawgrass (-18)
Runner(s) Up: Colin Montgomerie, Tommy Tolles
ROOKIE OF THE YEAR – Tiger Woods
U.S. AMATEUR CHAMPION – Tiger Woods, Pumpkin Ridge GC (38 Holes)
Runner Up: Steve Scott
BRITISH AMATEUR CHAMPION – Warren Bladon, Turnberry (1 up)
Runner Up: Roger Beames

HIGHLIGHTS

- The PGA Championship's playoff took place on number 18 of Valhalla, a par 5. Kenny Perry's fourth shot was a chip that never made it to the green, while Mark Brooks made it on the green in two and two-putted for an effortless birdie to win.

- Tiger Woods became the first player to win the U.S. Amateur three years in a row.

1997

PLAYER OF THE YEAR – Tiger Woods
LEADING MONEY WINNER – Tiger Woods $2,066,833

MAJOR WINNERS:

MASTERS – Tiger Woods, Augusta National (-18)
Runner(s) Up: Tom Kite (-6)
U.S. OPEN – Ernie Els, Congressional (-4)
Runner(s) Up: Colin Montgomerie (-3)
THE OPEN – Justin Leonard, Royal Troon (-12)
Runner(s) Up: Darren Clarke, Jesper Parnevik (-9)
PGA CHAMPIONSHIP – Davis Love III, Winged Foot (-11)
Runner(s) Up: Justin Leonard (-6)
THE PLAYERS – Steve Elkington, TPC Sawgrass (-16)
Runner(s) Up: Scott Hoch (-9)
ROOKIE OF THE YEAR – Stewart Cink
U.S. AMATEUR CHAMPION – Matt Kuchar, Cog Hill G&CC (2&1)
Runner Up: Joel Kribel
BRITISH AMATEUR CHAMPION – Craig Watson, Royal St. George's (3&2)
Runner Up: Trevor Immelman

HIGHLIGHTS

- Tiger Woods won the first major he ever played, The Masters. He became the first major winner from African or Asian descent.
- The Masters that Woods won was also marked by two more records: the youngest Masters winner, at 21 years, 104 days, and his 12-stroke win margin.

1998

PLAYER OF THE YEAR – Mark O'Meara
LEADING MONEY WINNER – David Duval $2,591,031

MAJOR WINNERS:

MASTERS – Mark O'Meara, Augusta National (-9)
Runner(s) Up: Fred Couples, David Duval (-8)
U.S. OPEN – Lee Janzen, Olympic Club (E)
Runner(s) Up: Payne Stewart (+1)
THE OPEN – Mark O'Meara, Royal Birkdale (E)
Runner(s) Up: Brian Watts (E)
PGA CHAMPIONSHIP – Vijay Singh, Sahalee (-9)
Runner(s) Up: Steve Stricker (-7)
THE PLAYERS – Justin Leonard, TPC Sawgrass (-10)
Runner(s) Up: Glen Day, Tom Lehman (-8)
ROOKIE OF THE YEAR – Steve Flesch
U.S. AMATEUR CHAMPION – Hank Kuehne, Oak Hill CC (2&1)
Runner Up: Tom McKnight
BRITISH AMATEUR CHAMPION – Sergio Garcia, Muirfield (7&6)
Runner Up: Craig Williams

HIGHLIGHTS

- THE OPEN playoff still utilized a four-hole playoff format, where Mark O'Meara birdied the first hole in the sequence and parred the rest to shoot -1 and win against Watts' +1 finish.
- Mark O'Meara became a first-time major winner at age 41 at The Masters. He did it in a rare fashion, by birdieing his final hole.

1999

PLAYER OF THE YEAR – Tiger Woods
LEADING MONEY WINNER – Tiger Woods $6,616,585

MAJOR WINNERS:

MASTERS – Jose Maria Olazabal, Augusta National (-8)
Runner(s) Up: Davis Love III (-6)
U.S. OPEN – Payne Stewart, Pinehurst No.2 (-1)
Runner(s) Up: Phil Mickelson (E)
THE OPEN – Paul Lawrie, Carnoustie (+6)
Runner(s) Up: Justin Leonard, Jean Van de Velde (+6)
PGA CHAMPIONSHIP – Tiger Woods, Medinah (-11)
Runner(s) Up: Sergio Garcia (-10)
THE PLAYERS – David Duval, TPC Sawgrass (-3)
Runner(s) Up: Scott Gump (-1)
ROOKIE OF THE YEAR – Carlos Franco
U.S. AMATEUR CHAMPION – David Gossett, Pebble Beach (9&8)
Runner Up: Sung Yoon Kim
BRITISH AMATEUR CHAMPION – Graeme Storm, Royal County Down (7&6)
Runner Up: Aran Wainwright

HIGHLIGHTS

- At THE OPEN, all three players got off to bad starts in the four-hole playoff. Lawrie and Leonard were +2 after 15 and 16, and Van de Velde, who blew a final round lead with a triple-bogey on the final hole, was +3. Lawrie was the only one able to come back, finishing with two birdies to get back to even, while the others finished at +3.
- The World Golf Championships (WGC) sequence of events begin. They provide four events.

2000

PLAYER OF THE YEAR – Tiger Woods

LEADING MONEY WINNER – Tiger Woods $9,188,321

MAJOR WINNERS:

MASTERS – Vijay Singh, Augusta National (-10)

Runner(s) Up: Ernie Els (-7)

U.S. OPEN – Tiger Woods, Pebble Beach (-12)

Runner(s) Up: Ernie Els, Miguel Angel Jimenez (+3)

THE OPEN – Tiger Woods, St. Andrews (-19)

Runner(s) Up: Thomas Bjorn, Ernie Els (-11)

PGA CHAMPIONSHIP – Tiger Woods, Valhalla (-18)

Runner(s) Up: Bob May (-18)

THE PLAYERS – Hal Sutton, TPC Sawgrass (-10)

Runner(s) Up: Tiger Woods (-9)

ROOKIE OF THE YEAR – Michael Clark II

U.S. AMATEUR CHAMPION – Jeff Quinney, Baltusrol GC (39 holes)

Runner Up: James Driscoll

BRITISH AMATEUR CHAMPION – Mikko Ilonen, Royal Liverpool (2&1)
Runner Up: Christian Reimbold

HIGHLIGHTS

- Three pars in the 3-hole aggregate playoff were not good enough for Bob May to defeat Tiger Woods at the PGA Championship, as Woods made one birdie and two pars to win by one.
- This was Tiger Woods' most dominant year, and the most dominant year of any Tour player ever. He won 11 of 25 events, three of them majors, and set all-time scoring records at each one.

2001

PLAYER OF THE YEAR – Tiger Woods
LEADING MONEY WINNER – Tiger Woods $5,687,777

MAJOR WINNERS:

MASTERS – Tiger Woods, Augusta National (-16)
Runner(s) Up: David Duval (-14)
U.S. OPEN – Retief Goosen, Southern Hills (-4)
Runner(s) Up: Mark Brooks (-4)
THE OPEN – David Duval, Royal Lytham & St. Annes (-10)
Runner(s) Up: Niclas Fasth (-7)
PGA CHAMPIONSHIP – David Toms, Atlanta Athletic Club (-15)
Runner(s) Up: Phil Mickelson (-14)
THE PLAYERS – Tiger Woods, TPC Sawgrass (-14)
Runner(s) Up: Vijay Singh (-13)
ROOKIE OF THE YEAR – Charles Howell III

U.S. AMATEUR CHAMPION – Bubba Dickerson, East Lake GC
(1 up)
Runner Up: Robert Hamilton
BRITISH AMATEUR CHAMPION – Michael Hoey, Prestwick
(1 up)
Runner Up: Ian Campbell

HIGHLIGHTS

- Retief Goosen won in a Monday 18-hole playoff at the U.S. OPEN over Mark Brooks with a 70 (E) over Brooks' 72 (+2).
- The year Tiger completed the "Tiger Slam," named because he held all four major titles at the same time, but not in the same year. He is the only person to have accomplished this.

2002

PLAYER OF THE YEAR – Tiger Woods
LEADING MONEY WINNER – Tiger Woods $6,912,625

MAJOR WINNERS:

MASTERS – Tiger Woods, Augusta National (-12)
Runner(s) Up: Retief Goosen (-9)
U.S. OPEN – Tiger Woods, Bethpage Black (-3)
Runner(s) Up: Phil Mickelson (E)
THE OPEN – Ernie Els, Muirfield (-6)
Runner(s) Up: Stuart Appleby, Steve Elkington, Thomas Levet (-6)
PGA CHAMPIONSHIP – Rich Beem, Hazeltine (-10)
Runner(s) Up: Tiger Woods (-9)
THE PLAYERS – Craig Perks, TPC Sawgrass (-8)

Runner(s) Up: Stephen Ames (-6)

ROOKIE OF THE YEAR – Jonathan Byrd

U.S. AMATEUR CHAMPION – Ricky Barnes, Oakland Hills CC (2&1)

Runner Up: Hunter Mahan

BRITISH AMATEUR CHAMPION – Alejandro Larrazabal, Royal Porthcawl (1 up)

Runner Up: Martin Sell

HIGHLIGHTS

- At THE OPEN, a four-man playoff was needed for the first time in its history. Ernie Els and Thomas Levet were still tied after the 4-hole aggregate playoff, so they headed to number 18 for sudden death. Els parred the hole to win over Levet, who made bogey.

2003

PLAYER OF THE YEAR – Tiger Woods

LEADING MONEY WINNER – Vijay Singh $7,573,907

MAJOR WINNERS:

MASTERS – Mike Weir. Augusta National (-7)

Runner(s) Up: Len Mattiace (-7)

U.S. OPEN – Jim Furyk, Olympia Fields (-8)

Runner(s) Up: Stephen Leaney (-5)

THE OPEN – Ben Curtis, Royal St. Georges (-1)

Runner(s) Up: Thomas Bjorn, Vijay Singh (E)

PGA CHAMPIONSHIP – Shaun Micheel, Oak Hill (-4)

Runner(s) Up: Chad Campbell (-2)

THE PLAYERS – Davis Love III, TPC Sawgrass (-17)
Runner(s) Up: Jay Haas, Padraig Harrington (-11)
ROOKIE OF THE YEAR – Ben Curtis
U.S. AMATEUR CHAMPION – Nick Flanagan, Oakmont CC (37 holes)
Runner Up: Casey Wittenberg
BRITISH AMATEUR CHAMPION – Gary Wolstenholme, Royal Troon (6&5)
Runner Up: Raphael De Sousa

HIGHLIGHTS

- Mike Weir became the first Canadian to win a major event, and the first lefty to win The Masters. His success occurred when he made a bogey on the first playoff hole against Len Mattiace, who had made a double bogey.
- The President's Cup is tied for the first time after a playoff is called off due to darkness.

2004

PLAYER OF THE YEAR –Vijay Singh
LEADING MONEY WINNER – Vijay Singh $10,905,166

MAJOR WINNERS:

MASTERS – Phil Mickelson, Augusta National (-9)
Runner(s) Up: Ernie Els (-8)
U.S. OPEN – Retief Goosen, Shinnecock Hills (-4)
Runner(s) Up: Phil Mickelson (-2)
THE OPEN – Todd Hamilton, Royal Troon (-10)

Runner(s) Up: Ernie Els (-10)

PGA CHAMPIONSHIP – Vijay Singh, Whistling Straits (-8)

Runner(s) Up: Chris DiMarco, Justin Leonard (-8)

THE PLAYERS – Adam Scott, TPC Sawgrass (-12)

Runner(s) Up: Padraig Harrington (-11)

ROOKIE OF THE YEAR – Todd Hamilton

U.S. AMATEUR CHAMPION – Ryan Moore, Winged Foot GC (2 up)

Runner Up: Luke List

BRITISH AMATEUR CHAMPION – Stuart Wilson, St. Andrews (4&3)

Runner Up: Lee Corfield

HIGHLIGHTS

- Vijay Singh shot a birdie-free 76 in the final round of the PGA Championship, but still made it into the 3-hole playoff, where he made his first birdie of the day on the first hole (#10) and parred the others, forcing his two competitors to make a birdie, which neither did.
- Els lost THE OPEN after shooting four rounds in the 60's again, losing in a 4-hole playoff by one.

2005

PLAYER OF THE YEAR – Tiger Woods

LEADING MONEY WINNER – Tiger Woods $10,628,024

MAJOR WINNERS:

MASTERS – Tiger Woods, Augusta National (-12)

Runner(s) Up: Chris DiMarco (-12)

U.S. OPEN – Michael Campbell, Pinehurst No. 2 (E)

Runner(s) Up: Tiger Woods (+2)

THE OPEN – Tiger Woods, St. Andrews (-14)

Runner(s) Up: Colin Montgomerie (-9)

PGA CHAMPIONSHIP – Phil Mickelson, Baltusrol (-4)

Runner(s) Up: Thomas Bjorn, Steve Elkington (-3)

THE PLAYERS – Fred Funk, TPC Sawgrass (-9)

Runner(s) Up: Luke Donald, Tom Lehman, Scott Verplank (-8)

ROOKIE OF THE YEAR – Sean O'Hair

U.S. AMATEUR CHAMPION – Edoardo Molinari, Merion GC (4&3)

Runner Up: Dillon Dougherty

BRITISH AMATEUR CHAMPION – Brian McElhinney, Royal Birkdale (5&4)

Runner Up: John Gallagher

HIGHLIGHTS

- Tiger won The Masters on the first playoff hole with a birdie. This was Chris DiMarco's second major playoff defeat in a row.
- Woods ended his record of consecutive PGA Tour cuts made at the EDS Byron Nelson Championship. He finished with 142 cuts made in a row.

2006

PLAYER OF THE YEAR – Tiger Woods

LEADING MONEY WINNER – Tiger Woods $9,941,563

MAJOR WINNERS:

MASTERS – Phil Mickelson, Augusta National (-7)

Runner(s) Up: Tim Clark (-5)

U.S. OPEN – Geoff Ogilvy, Winged Foot (+5)

Runner(s) Up: Jim Furyk, Phil Mickelson, Colin Montgomerie (+6)

THE OPEN – Tiger Woods, Royal Liverpool (-18)

Runner(s) Up: Chris DiMarco (-16)

PGA CHAMPIONSHIP – Tiger Woods, Medinah (-18)

Runner(s) Up: Shaun Micheel (-13)

THE PLAYERS – Stephen Ames, TPC Sawgrass (-14)

Runner(s) Up: Retief Goosen (-8)

ROOKIE OF THE YEAR – Trevor Immelman

U.S. AMATEUR CHAMPION – Richie Ramsay, Hazeltine (4&2)

Runner Up: John Kelly

BRITISH AMATEUR CHAMPION – Julien Guerrier, Royal St. George's (4&3)

Runner Up: Adam Gee

HIGHLIGHTS

- The Ryder Cup was played in Ireland for the first time ever.
- PGA Tour announced more details for the FedEx Cup that was set to begin in 2007. The first-place prize was estimated at $10 million.

2007

PLAYER OF THE YEAR – Tiger Woods

LEADING MONEY WINNER – Tiger Woods $10,867,052

FEDEX CUP CHAMPION – Tiger Woods

MAJOR WINNERS:

MASTERS – Zach Johnson, Augusta National (+1)

Runner(s) Up: Retief Goosen, Rory Sabbatini, Tiger Woods (+3)

U.S. OPEN – Angel Cabrera, Oakmont (+5)

Runner(s) Up: Jim Furyk, Tiger Woods (+6)

THE OPEN – Padraig Harrington, Carnoustie (-7)

Runner(s) Up: Sergio Garcia (-7)

PGA CHAMPIONSHIP – Tiger Woods, Southern Hills (-8)

Runner(s) Up: Woody Austin (-6)

THE PLAYERS – Phil Mickelson, TPC Sawgrass (-11)

Runner(s) Up: Sergio Garcia (-9)

ROOKIE OF THE YEAR – Brandt Snedeker

U.S. AMATEUR CHAMPION – Colt Knost, The Olympic Club (2&1)

Runner Up: Michael Thompson

BRITISH AMATEUR CHAMPION – Drew Weaver, Royal Lytham & St. Annes (2&1)

Runner Up: Tim Stewart

HIGHLIGHTS

- At THE OPEN, Padraig Harrington had a 2-stroke advantage with one hole to go in the 4-hole aggregate playoff, so he played number 18 safe. Harrington made his safe bogey, as Garcia's birdie putt to tie, burned the edge. They finished E and +1, respectively, for the four holes.

2008

PLAYER OF THE YEAR – Padraig Harrington

LEADING MONEY WINNER – Vijay Singh $6,601,094

FEDEX CUP CHAMPION – Vijay Singh

MAJOR WINNERS:

MASTERS – Trevor Immelman, Augusta National (-8)

Runner(s) Up: Tiger Woods (-5)

U.S. OPEN – Tiger Woods, Torrey Pines (-1)

Runner(s) Up: Rocco Mediate (-1)

THE OPEN – Padraig Harrington, Royal Birkdale (+3)

Runner(s) Up: Ian Poulter (+7)

PGA CHAMPIONSHIP – Padraig Harrington, Oakland Hills (-3)

Runner(s) Up: Ben Curtis, Sergio Garcia (-1)

THE PLAYERS – Sergio Garcia, TPC Sawgrass (-5)

Runner(s) Up: Paul Goydos (-5)

ROOKIE OF THE YEAR – Andres Romero

U.S. AMATEUR CHAMPION – Danny Lee, Pinehurst No. 2 (5&4)

Runner Up: Drew Kittleson

BRITISH AMATEUR CHAMPION – Reinier Saxton, Turnberry (3&2)

Runner Up: Tommy Fleetwood

HIGHLIGHTS

- Tiger Woods showing at the U.S. OPEN included birdies on number 18 on Sunday to force a playoff, and again, on Monday to make it to sudden death. Woods and Mediate tied with 71 (E) after the 18-hole playoff, and Woods parred the sudden death hole to win over Mediate's bogey.

2009

PLAYER OF THE YEAR – Tiger Woods

LEADING MONEY WINNER – Tiger Woods $10,508,163

FEDEX CUP CHAMPION – Tiger Woods

MAJOR WINNERS:

MASTERS – Angel Cabrera, Augusta National (-12)

Runner(s) Up: Chad Campbell, Kenny Perry (-12)

U.S. OPEN – Lucas Glover, Bethpage Black (-4)

Runner(s) Up: Ricky Barnes, David Duval, Phil Mickelson (-2)

THE OPEN – Stewart Cink, Turnberry (-2)

Runner(s) Up: Tom Watson (-2)

PGA CHAMPIONSHIP – Y.E. Yang, Hazeltine (-8)

Runner(s) Up: Tiger Woods (-5)

THE PLAYERS – Henrik Stenson, TPC Sawgrass (-12)

Runner(s) Up: Ian Poulter (-8)

ROOKIE OF THE YEAR – Marc Leishman

U.S. AMATEUR CHAMPION – An-Byeong Hun, Southern Hills CC (7&5)

Runner Up: Ben Martin

BRITISH AMATEUR CHAMPION – Matteo Manassero, Formby (4&3)

Runner Up: Sam Hutsby

HIGHLIGHTS

- At The Masters, a 3-way playoff was to decide the champion. Chad Campbell was out after the first sudden death hole and then Angel Cabrera made a par on the second to edge out Perry.
- Stewart Cink won by a surprising six strokes in the 4-hole play-off at THE OPEN over Tom Watson.

2010

PLAYER OF THE YEAR – Jim Furyk

LEADING MONEY WINNER – Matt Kuchar $4,910,477

FEDEX CUP CHAMPION – Jim Furyk

MAJOR WINNERS:

MASTERS – Phil Mickelson, Augusta National (-16)

Runner(s) Up: Lee Westwood (-13)

U.S. OPEN – Graeme McDowell, Pebble Beach Golf Links (E)

Runner(s) Up: Gregory Havret (+1)

THE OPEN – Louis Oosthuizen, St. Andrews (-16)

Runner(s) Up: Lee Westwood (-9)

PGA CHAMPIONSHIP – Martin Kaymer, Whistling Straits (-11)

Runner(s) Up: Bubba Watson (-11)

THE PLAYERS – Tim Clark, TPC Sawgrass (-16)

Runner(s) Up: Robert Allenby (-15)

ROOKIE OF THE YEAR – Rickie Fowler

U.S. AMATEUR – Peter Uihlein, Chambers Bay (4&2)

Runner Up: David Chung

BRITISH AMATEUR – Jin Jeong, Muirfield (5&4)

Runner Up: James Byrne

HIGHLIGHTS

- Dustin Johnson was the victim of a 2-stroke penalty at the PGA after he grounded his club in an unmapped bunker that he had assumed was a waste bunker (would have been no penalty). As a result, he missed out on a 3-hole playoff where Martin Kaymer defeated Bubba Watson.

2011

PLAYER OF THE YEAR – Luke Donald

LEADING MONEY WINNER – Luke Donald $6,683,214
FEDEX CUP CHAMPION – Bill Haas

MAJOR WINNERS:

MASTERS – Charl Schwartzel, Augusta National (-14)
Runner(s) Up: Jason Day, Adam Scott (-12)
U.S. OPEN – Rory McIlroy, Congressional CC (-16)
Runner(s) Up: Jason Day (-8)
THE OPEN – Darren Clarke, Royal St. George's (-5)
Runner(s) Up: Phil Mickelson, Dustin Johnson (-2)
PGA CHAMPIONSHIP – Keegan Bradley, Atlanta Athletic Club (-8)
Runner(s) Up: Jason Dufner (-8)
THE PLAYERS – K.J. Choi, TPC Sawgrass (-13)
Runner(s) Up: David Toms (-13)
ROOKIE OF THE YEAR – Keegan Bradley
U.S. AMATEUR – Kelly Kraft, Erin Hills (2 Up)
Runner Up: Patrick Cantlay
BRITISH AMATEUR – Bryden Macpherson, Hillside GC (3&2)
Runner Up: Michael Stewart

HIGHLIGHTS

- Keegan Bradley won the PGA Championship, which was his first major appearance. He defeated Jason Dufner in the 3-hole cumulative playoff -1 to E.
- Three different players assumed world number 1 golfer during the year.

2012

PLAYER OF THE YEAR – Rory McIlroy

LEADING MONEY WINNER – Rory McIlroy $8,047,952
FEDEX CUP CHAMPION – Brandt Snedeker

MAJOR WINNERS:

MASTERS – Bubba Watson, Augusta National (-10)
Runner(s) Up: Louis Oosthuizen (-10)
U.S. OPEN – Webb Simpson, The Olympic Club (+1)
Runner(s) Up: Michael Thompson, Graeme McDowell (+2)
THE OPEN – Ernie Els, Royal Lytham & St. Annes (-7)
Runner(s) Up: Adam Scott (-6)
PGA CHAMPIONSHIP – Rory McIlroy, The Ocean Course at
Kiawah Island (-13)
Runner(s) Up: David Lynn (-5)
THE PLAYERS – Matt Kuchar, TPC Sawgrass (-13)
Runner(s) Up: Ben Curtis, Rickie Fowler, Zach Johnson, Martin Laird (-11)
ROOKIE OF THE YEAR – John Huh
U.S. AMATEUR – Steven Fox, Cherry Hills CC (37 holes)
Runner Up: Michael Weaver
BRITISH AMATEUR – Alan Dunbar, Royal Troon (1 Up)
Runner Up: Matthias Schwab

HIGHLIGHTS

- Bubba Watson won his first major title at The Masters this year, requiring two playoff holes to beat Louis Oosthuizen.
- Rory McIlroy and Luke Donald exchanged world number one status seven times.

2013

PLAYER OF THE YEAR – Tiger Woods

LEADING MONEY WINNER – Tiger Woods $8,553,439
FEDEX CUP CHAMPION – Henrik Stenson

MAJOR WINNERS:

MASTERS – Adam Scott, Augusta National (-9)
Runner(s) Up: Angel Cabrera (-9)
U.S. OPEN – Justin Rose, Merion GC (+1)
Runner(s) Up: Jason Day, Phil Mickelson (+3)
THE OPEN – Phil Mickelson, Muirfield (-3)
Runner(s) Up: Henrik Stenson (E)
PGA CHAMPIONSHIP – Jason Dufner, Oak Hill CC (-10)
Runner(s) Up: Jim Furyk (-8)
THE PLAYERS – Tiger Woods, TPC Sawgrass (-13)
Runner(s) Up: Kevin Streelman, David Lingmerth, Jeff Maggert (-11)
ROOKIE OF THE YEAR – Jordan Spieth
U.S. AMATEUR – Matthew Fitzpatrick, The Country Club (4&3)
Runner Up: Oliver Goss
BRITISH AMATEUR – Garrick Porteous, Royal Cinque Ports (6&5)
Runner Up: Toni Hakula

HIGHLIGHTS

- Adam Scott became the first Australian to win The Masters, defeating playing competitor Angel Cabrera on the second playoff hole with a birdie.
- Jordan Spieth won the John Deere Classic, as the first teenager to win a Tour event since 1931.

2014

PLAYER OF THE YEAR – Rory McIlroy

LEADING MONEY WINNER – Rory McIlroy $8,280,096

FEDEX CUP CHAMPION – Billy Horschel

MAJOR WINNERS:

MASTERS – Bubba Watson, Augusta National (-8)

Runner(s) Up: Jonas Blixt, Jordan Spieth (-5)

U.S. OPEN – Martin Kaymer, Pinehurst No. 2 (-9)

Runner(s) Up: Erik Compton, Rickie Fowler (-1)

THE OPEN – Rory McIlroy, Royal Liverpool (-17)

Runner(s) Up: Sergio Garcia, Rickie Fowler (-15)

PGA CHAMPIONSHIP – Rory McIlroy, Valhalla GC (-16)

Runner(s) Up: Phil Mickelson (-15)

THE PLAYERS – Martin Kaymer, TPC Sawgrass (-13)

Runner(s) Up: Jim Furyk (-12)

ROOKIE OF THE YEAR – Chesson Hadley

U.S. AMATEUR – Gunn Yang, Atlanta Athletic Club (2&1)

Runner Up: Corey Conners

BRITISH AMATEUR – Bradley Neil, Royal Portrush (2&1)

Runner Up: Zander Lombard

HIGHLIGHTS

- Miguel Ángel Jiménez broke his own record as oldest player to win a European Tour event at 50 years and 133 days.

2015

PLAYER OF THE YEAR – Jordan Spieth

LEADING MONEY WINNER – Jordan Spieth $12,030,465

FEDEX CUP CHAMPION – Jordan Spieth

MAJOR WINNERS:

MASTERS – Jordan Spieth, Augusta National (-18)

Runner(s) Up: Phil Mickelson, Justin Rose (-14)

U.S. OPEN – Jordan Spieth, Chambers Bay (-5)

Runner(s) Up: Louis Oosthuizen, Dustin Johnson (-4)

THE OPEN – Zach Johnson, St. Andrews (-15)

Runner(s) Up: Louis Oosthuizen, Marc Leishman (-15)

PGA CHAMPIONSHIP – Jason Day, Whistling Straits (-20)

Runner(s) Up: Jordan Spieth (-17)

THE PLAYERS – Rickie Fowler, TPC Sawgrass (-12)

Runner(s) Up: Sergio Garcia, Kevin Kisner (-12)

ROOKIE OF THE YEAR – Daniel Berger

U.S. AMATEUR – Bryson DeChambeau, Olympia Fields CC (7&6)

Runner Up: Derek Bard

BRITISH AMATEUR – Romain Langasque, Carnoustie (4&2)

Runner Up: Grant Forrest

HIGHLIGHTS

- The Claret Jug was won by Zach Johnson when Louis Oosthuizen failed to make his putt on the fourth and final hole of the 4-hole aggregate playoff.
- World golf number one changed hands eight times this year.

2016

PLAYER OF THE YEAR – Dustin Johnson

LEADING MONEY WINNER – Dustin Johnson $9,365,185

FEDEX CUP CHAMPION – Rory McIlroy

MAJOR WINNERS:

MASTERS – Danny Willett, Augusta National (-5)

Runner(s) Up: Lee Westwood, Jordan Spieth (-2)

U.S. OPEN – Dustin Johnson, Oakmont CC (-4)

Runner(s) Up: Jim Furyk, Scott Piercy, Shane Lowry (-1)

THE OPEN – Henrik Stenson, Royal Troon (-20)

Runner(s) Up: Phil Mickelson (-17)

PGA CHAMPIONSHIP – Jimmy Walker, Baltusrol GC (-14)

Runner(s) Up: Jason Day (-13)

THE PLAYERS – Jason Day, TPC Sawgrass (-15)

Runner(s) Up: Kevin Chappell (-11)

ROOKIE OF THE YEAR – Emiliano Grillo

U.S. AMATEUR – Curtis Luck, Oakland Hills CC (6&4)

Runner Up: Brad Dalke

BRITISH AMATEUR – Scott Gregory, Royal Porthcawl (2&1)

Runner Up: Robert MacIntyre

HIGHLIGHTS

* Jim Furyk shot a 58 (-12) in the final round of the Travelers Championship. This was the lowest round ever shot in a PGA Tour event and made Furyk the only Tour player to break 60 on two different occasions.

2017

PLAYER OF THE YEAR –Justin Thomas

LEADING MONEY WINNER – Justin Thomas $9,921,560

FEDEX CUP CHAMPION – Justin Thomas

MAJOR WINNERS:

MASTERS – Sergio Garcia, Augusta National (-9)

Runner(s) Up: Justin Rose (-9)

U.S. OPEN – Brooks Koepka, Erin Hills (-16)

Runner(s) Up: Brian Harman, Hideki Matsuyama (-12)

THE OPEN – Jordan Spieth, Royal Birkdale (-12)

Runner(s) Up: Matt Kuchar (-9)

PGA CHAMPIONSHIP – Justin Thomas, Quail Hollow Club (-8)

Runner(s) Up: Francesco Molinari, Louis Oosthuizen, Patrick Reed (-6)

THE PLAYERS – Kim Si-woo, TPC Sawgrass (-10)

Runner(s) Up: Louis Oosthuizen, Ian Poulter (-7)

ROOKIE OF THE YEAR – Xander Schauffele

U.S. AMATEUR – Doc Redman, Riviera CC (37 holes)

Runner Up: Doug Ghim

BRITISH AMATEUR – Harry Ellis, Royal St. George's (38 holes)

Runner Up: Dylan Perry

HIGHLIGHTS

- After 74 major starts, Sergio Garcia finally won his first major at The Masters. After Rose struggled on the first playoff hole, Garcia had two putts for the win, but he drained his first putt.

Chapter 11:
LPGA TOUR HIGHLIGHTS BY YEAR

1946
MAJOR WINNERS:

U.S. OPEN – Patty Berg, Spokane CC (5&4)

Runner(s) Up: Betty Jameson

TITLEHOLDERS – Louise Suggs(a), Augusta CC (+14)

Runner(s) Up: Eileen Stulb (+16)

U.S. WOMEN'S AMATEUR – Babe Zaharias, Southern Hills CC (11&9)

Runner Up: Clara Sherman

HIGHLIGHTS

* Inaugural U.S. Women's Open, only year played with match play. Conducted by Women's Professional Golfers Association (1946-1948).

1947
MAJOR WINNERS:

U.S. OPEN – Betty Jameson, Starmount Forest CC (-9)

Runner(s) Up: Sally Sessions(a), Polly Riley(a) (-3)

TITLEHOLDERS – Babe Didrikson Zaharias, Augusta CC (+4)

Runner(s) Up: Dorothy Kirby(a) (+9)

U.S. WOMEN'S AMATEUR CHAMPION – Louise Suggs, Franklin Hills CC (2 up)

Runner Up: Dorothy Kirby

- Babe Zaharias becomes the first American golfer to win the British Women's Amateur.

1948

MAJOR WINNERS:

U.S. OPEN – Babe Didrikson Zaharias, Atlantic City CC (E)
Runner(s) Up: Betty Hicks (+8)
TITLEHOLDERS – Patty Berg, Augusta CC (+8)
Runner(s) Up: Peggy Kirk, Babe Didrikson Zaharias (+9)
U.S. WOMEN'S AMATEUR – Grace Lencyzk, Del Monte G&CC (4&3)
Runner Up: Helen Sigel

HIGHLIGHTS
- Babe Zaharias wins the first of her three U.S. Opens.

1949

MAJOR WINNERS:

U.S. OPEN – Louise Suggs, Prince George's G&CC (-9)
Runner(s) Up: Babe Didrikson Zaharias (+5)
TITLEHOLDERS – Peggy Kirk(a), Augusta CC (-1)
Runner(s) Up: Patty Berg, Dorothy Kirby(a) (+1)
U.S. WOMEN'S AMATEUR – Dorothy Porter, Merion GC (3&2)
Runner Up: Dorothy Kielty

HIGHLIGHTS

- First Year U.S. Women's Open conducted by LPGA (1949-1952)
- Louise Suggs wins the U.S. Open by a record 14 strokes.

1950

LEADING MONEY WINNER – Babe Didrikson Zaharias $14,800

MAJOR WINNERS:

U.S. OPEN – Babe Didrikson Zaharias, Rolling Hills CC (-9)
Runner(s) Up: Betsy Rawls(a) (E)
TITLEHOLDERS – Babe Didrikson Zaharias, Augusta CC (+10)
Runner(s) Up: Claire Doran(a) (+18)
WESTERN OPEN – Babe Didrikson Zaharias, Cherry Hills CC (5&3)
Runner(s) Up: Peggy Kirk
U.S. WOMEN'S AMATEUR – Beverly Hanson, Atlanta Athletic Club (6&4)
Runner Up: Mae Murray

HIGHLIGHTS

- First Year of Money records
- LPGA founded, among the founders are Babe Zaharias, Louise Suggs, and Patty Berg.
- Western Open Match Play 1930-1954

1951

LEADING MONEY WINNER – Babe Didrikson Zaharias $15,087

MAJOR WINNERS:

U.S. OPEN – Betsy Rawls, Druid Hills GC (+5)

Runner(s) Up: Louise Suggs (+10)

TITLEHOLDER'S – Pat O'Sullivan(a), Augusta CC (+13)

Runner(s) Up: Beverly Hanson(a) (+15)

WESTERN OPEN – Patty Berg, Whitemarsh Valley CC (2 up)

Runner Up: Pat O'Sullivan(a)

U.S. WOMEN'S AMATEUR – Dorothy Kirby, Town & CC (2&1)

Runner Up: Claire Doran

HIGHLIGHTS

- Betsy Rawls wins the first of her eight major championships at the U.S. Open.
- Amateurs are the victor and runner-up in the Titleholders Championship.

1952

LEADING MONEY WINNER – Betsy Rawls $14,505

MAJOR WINNERS:

U.S. OPEN – Louise Suggs, Bala GC (+8)

Runner(s) Up: Marlene Bauer, Betty Jameson (+15)

TITLEHOLDER'S – Babe Didrikson Zaharias, Augusta CC (+11)

Runner(s) Up: Betsy Rawls (+18)

WESTERN OPEN – Betsy Rawls, Skokie CC (1 up)

Runner Up: Betty Jameson

U.S. WOMEN'S AMATEUR – Jacqueline Pung, Waverley CC (2&1)

Runner Up: Shirley McFedters

HIGHLIGHTS

- Mickey Wright becomes known on the golf scene after winning the U.S. Girl's Junior.
- Patty Berg shoots a then LPGA-record 64 for 18 holes.

1953

LEADING MONEY WINNER – Louise Suggs $19,816

MAJOR WINNERS:

U.S. OPEN – Betsy Rawls, CC of Rochester (+6)

Runner(s) Up: Jacqueline Pung (+6)

TITLEHOLDERS – Patty Berg, Augusta CC (+6)

Runner(s) Up: Betsy Rawls (+15)

WESTERN OPEN – Louise Suggs, Capital City Club (6&5)

Runner Up: Patty Berg

U.S. WOMEN'S AMATEUR – Mary Lena Faulk, Rhode Island CC (3&2)

Runner Up: Polly Riley

HIGHLIGHTS

- First year U.S. Women's Open conducted by USGA.
- Betsy Rawls wins the U.S. Women's Open in a playoff over Jackie Pung, 71-77

1954

LEADING MONEY WINNER – Patty Berg $16,011

MAJOR WINNERS:

U.S. OPEN – Babe Didrikson Zaharias, Salem CC (+3)
Runner(s) Up: Betty Hicks (+15)
TITLEHOLDERS – Louise Suggs, Augusta CC (+5)
Runner(s) Up: Patty Berg (+12)
WESTERN OPEN – Betty Jameson, Glen Flora CC (6&5)
Runner Up: Louise Suggs
U.S. WOMEN'S AMATEUR – Barbara Romack, Allegheny CC (4&2)
Runner Up: Mickey Wright

HIGHLIGHTS

- Babe Zaharias wins the U.S. Open a year after undergoing cancer surgery.

1955

LEADING MONEY WINNER – Patty Berg $16,462

MAJOR WINNERS:

U.S. OPEN – Fay Crocker, Wichita CC (+11)
Runner(s) Up: Mary Lena Faulk, Louise Suggs (+15)
LPGA – Beverly Hanson, Orchard Ridge CC (4&3)

Runner(s) Up: Louise Suggs (-2)

TITLEHOLDERS – Patty Berg, Augusta CC (+3)

Runner(s) Up: Mary Lena Faulk (+5)

WESTERN OPEN – Patty Berg, Maple Bluff CC (E)

Runner(s) Up: Fay Crocker, Louise Suggs (+2)

U.S. WOMEN'S AMATEUR – Patricia Lesser, Myers Park CC (7&6)

Runner Up: Jane Nelson

HIGHLIGHTS

- First year of Women's PGA Championship – three rounds of stroke play followed by match play.
- Western Open was a stroke play major 1955-1967.

1956

LEADING MONEY WINNER – Marlene Hagge $20,235

MAJOR WINNERS:

U.S. OPEN – Kathy Cornelius, Northland CC (+7)

Runner(s) Up: Barbara McIntire(a) (+7)

LPGA – Marlene Hagge, Forest Lake CC (-9)

Runner(s) Up: Patty Berg (-9)

TITLEHOLDERS – Louise Suggs, Augusta CC (+14)

Runner(s) Up: Patty Berg (+15)

WESTERN OPEN – Beverly Hanson, Wakonda CC (E)

Runner(s) Up: Louise Suggs (+4)

U.S. WOMEN'S AMATEUR – Marlene Stewart, Meridian Hills CC (2&1)

Runner Up: JoAnne Gunderson

HIGHLIGHTS

- Kathy Cornelius wins the U.S. Open in a playoff over amateur Barb McIntire, with a 75 to McIntire's 82.
- Marlene Hagge wins her only major over Patty Berg in a sudden death playoff at the Women's LPGA Championship with bogey on the first playoff hole.
- Mickey Wright wins the first of her 82 LPGA Tour victories.

1957

LEADING MONEY WINNER – Patty Berg $16,272

MAJOR WINNERS:

U.S. OPEN – Betsy Rawls, Winged Foot GC (+7)
Runner(s) Up: Patty Berg (+13)
LPGA – Louise Suggs, Churchill Valley CC (+5)
Runner(s) Up: Wiffi Smith (+8)
TITLEHOLDERS – Patty Berg, Augusta CC (+8)
Runner(s) Up: Anne Quast(a) (+11)
WESTERN OPEN – Patty Berg, Montgomery CC (-1)
Runner(s) Up: Wiffi Smith (E)
U.S. WOMEN'S AMATEUR – JoAnne Gunderson, Del Paso CC (8&6)
Runner Up: Ann Casey Johnstone

HIGHLIGHTS

- Jackie Pung posts the lowest score in the U.S. Open, but signs an incorrect scorecard and is disqualified.
- Mickey Wright shoots 104 in a round in the LPGA Tampa Women's Open, 24 strokes being attributed to an extra club in her bag for the first 12 holes.

1958

LEADING MONEY WINNER – Beverly Hanson $12,639

MAJOR WINNERS:
U.S. OPEN – Mickey Wright, Forest Lake CC (-2)
Runner(s) Up: Louise Suggs (+3)
LPGA – Mickey Wright, Churchill Valley CC (+8)
Runner(s) Up: Fay Crocker (+14)
TITLEHOLDERS – Beverly Hanson, Augusta CC (+11)
Runner(s) Up: Betty Dodd (+16)
WESTERN OPEN – Patty Berg, Kahkwa CC (+1)
Runner(s) Up: Beverly Hanson (+5)
U.S. WOMEN'S AMATEUR – Anne Quast, Wee Burn CC (3&2)
Runner Up: Barbara Romack

HIGHLIGHTS
- Kathy Whitworth defeats Mickey Wright in a playoff in the LPGA Lady Carling Open. With the win, Whitworth won her fourth straight event, tying Wright's record for most consecutive wins.

1959

LEADING MONEY WINNER – Betsy Rawls $26,774

MAJOR WINNERS:

U.S. OPEN – Mickey Wright, Churchill Valley CC (+7)

Runner(s) Up: Louise Suggs (+9)

LPGA – Betsy Rawls, Sheraton Hotel CC (-8)

Runner(s) Up: Patty Berg (-7)

TITLEHOLDERS – Louise Suggs, Augusta CC (+9)

Runner(s) Up: Betsy Rawls (+10)

WESTERN OPEN – Betsy Rawls, Ranier G&CC (-1)

Runner(s) Up: JoAnne Gunderson(a), Patty Berg (+5)

U.S. WOMEN'S AMATEUR – Barbara McIntire, Congressional CC (4&3)

Runner Up: Joanne Goodwin

HIGHLIGHTS

- Betsy Rawls wins ten times.
- Mickey Wright wins her second consecutive U.S. Open.

1960

LEADING MONEY WINNER – Louise Suggs $16,892

MAJOR WINNERS:

U.S. OPEN – Betsy Rawls, Worcester CC (+4)

Runner(s) Up: Joyce Ziske (+5)

LPGA – Mickey Wright, Sheraton Hotel CC (-4)

Runner(s) Up: Louise Suggs (-1)

TITLEHOLDERS – Fay Crocker, Augusta CC (+15)

Runner(s) Up: Kathy Cornelius (+22)

WESTERN OPEN – Joyce Ziske, Beverly CC (+9)

Runner(s) Up: Barbara Romack (+9)

U.S. WOMEN'S AMATEUR – JoAnne Gunderson, Tulsa CC (6&5)
Runner Up: Jean Ashley

HIGHLIGHTS
- Joyce Ziske wins the Western Open over Barbara Romack in a playoff on the second hole.
- Betsy Rawls wins her fourth U.S. Women's Open.

1961

LEADING MONEY WINNER – Mickey Wright $22,236

MAJOR WINNERS:
U.S. OPEN – Mickey Wright, Baltusrol GC (+5)
Runner(s) Up: Betsy Rawls (+11)
LPGA – Mickey Wright, Stardust CC, (+3)
Runner(s) Up: Louise Suggs (+12)
TITLEHOLDER'S – Mickey Wright, Augusta CC (+11)
Runner(s) Up: Patty Berg, Louise Suggs (+12)
WESTERN OPEN – Mary Lena Faulk, Belle Meade CC (-10)
Runner(s) Up: Betsy Rawls (-4)
U.S. WOMEN'S AMATEUR – Anne Sander, Tacoma C&GC (14&13)
Runner Up: Phyllis Preuss

HIGHLIGHTS
- Mickey Wright wins ten times, including three major championships.
- Louise Suggs wins the Palm Beach Par-3 invitational, a co-ed event. All competitors play from the same tees and among them, Sam Snead.

1962

LEADING MONEY WINNER – Mickey Wright $21,641

MAJOR WINNERS:

U.S. OPEN – Murle Lindstrom, Dunes G&BC (+13)

Runner(s) Up: Ruth Jessen, JoAnn Prentice (+15)

LPGA – Judy Kimball, Stardust CC (-2)

Runner(s) Up: Shirley Spork (+2)

TITLEHOLDERS – Mickey Wright, Augusta CC (+7)

Runner(s) Up: Ruth Jessen (+7)

WESTERN OPEN – Mickey Wright, Montgomery CC (+7)

Runner(s) Up: Mary Lena Faulk (+7)

ROOKIE OF THE YEAR – Mary Mills

U.S. WOMEN'S AMATEUR – JoAnne Carner, CC of Rochester (9&8)

Runner Up: Ann Baker

HIGHLIGHTS

- First year of Rookie of the Year award.
- Mickey Wright is victorious in playoffs for both the Titleholders Championship and the Western Open. In the Titleholders, she shoots a 69 to Ruth Jessen's 72 and in the Western Open on the fourth hole of a sudden-death playoff.

1963

LEADING MONEY WINNER – Mickey Wright $31,269

MAJOR WINNERS:

U.S. OPEN – Mary Mills, Kenwood CC (-3)

Runner(s) Up: Sandra Haynie, Louise Suggs (E)

LPGA – Mickey Wright, Stardust CC (+10)

Runner(s) Up: Lena Faulk, Mary Mills, Lousie Suggs (+12)

TITLEHOLDERS – Marilynn Smith, Augusta CC (E)

Runner(s) Up: Mickey Wright (E)

WESTERN OPEN – Mickey Wright, Maple Bluff CC (-4)

Runner(s) Up: Kathy Whitworth (+5)

ROOKIE OF THE YEAR – Clifford Ann Creed

U.S. WOMEN'S AMATEUR – Anne Sander, Taconic GC (2&1)

Runner Up: Peggy Conley

HIGHLIGHTS

- Mickey Wright wins a record 13 times on Tour.
- Marilynn Smith defeats Mickey Wright in a playoff for the Titleholders Championship with a par putt on the last hole of an 18-hole playoff to win by one stroke.

1964

LEADING MONEY WINNER – Mickey Wright $29,800

MAJOR WINNERS:

U.S. OPEN – Mickey Wright, San Diego CC (-2)

Runner(s) Up: Ruth Jessen (-2)

LPGA – Mary Mills, Stardust CC (-6)

Runner(s) Up: Mickey Wright (4)

TITLEHOLDERS – Marilynn Smith, Augusta CC (+1)

Runner(s) Up: Mickey Wright (+2)

WESTERN OPEN – Carol Mann, Scenic Hills CC (+8)

Runner(s) Up: Ruth Jessen, Judy Kimball (+10)

ROOKIE OF THE YEAR – Susie Berning

U.S. WOMEN'S AMATEUR – Barbara McIntire, Prairie Dunes CC (3&2)

Runner Up: JoAnne Carner

HIGHLIGHTS

- Mickey Wright wins the U.S. Open in a playoff, shooting 70 to Ruth Jessen's 72.
- Mickey Wright shoots the LPGA's lowest round at the time, a 62.

1965

LEADING MONEY WINNER – Kathy Whitworth $28,658

MAJOR WINNERS:

U.S. OPEN – Carol Mann, Atlantic City CC (+2)

Runner(s) Up: Kathy Cornelius (+4)

LPGA – Sandra Haynie, Stardust CC (-5)

Runner(s) Up: Clifford Ann Creed (-4)

TITLEHOLDERS – Kathy Whitworth, Augusta CC (-1)

Runner(s) Up: Peggy Wilson (+9)

WESTERN OPEN – Susie Maxwell, Beverly CC (-2)

Runner(s) Up: Marlene Hagge (+1)

ROOKIE OF THE YEAR – Margie Masters

U.S. WOMEN'S AMATEUR – Jean Ashley, Lakewood CC (5&4)

Runner Up: Anne Sander

HIGHLIGHTS

- The U.S. Women's Open becomes the first nationally televised women's event as its final round is broadcast.

1966

PLAYER OF THE YEAR – Kathy Whitworth
LEADING MONEY WINNER – Kathy Whitworth $33,517

MAJOR WINNERS:

U.S. OPEN – Sandra Spuzich, Hazeltine GC (+9)
Runner(s) Up: Carol Mann (+10)
LPGA – Gloria Ehret, Stardust CC (-2)
Runner(s) Up: Mickey Wright (+1)
TITLEHOLDERS – Kathy Whitworth, Augusta CC (+3)
Runner(s) Up: Judy Kimball, Mary Mills (+5)
WESTERN OPEN – Mickey Wright, Rainbow Springs CC (+2)
Runner(s) Up: Margie Masters, JoAnn Prentice (+3)
ROOKIE OF THE YEAR – Jan Ferraris
U.S. WOMEN'S AMATEUR – JoAnne Carner, Sewickley Heights GC (41 holes)
Runner Up: Marlene Streit

HIGHLIGHTS

- First year of Player of the Year Award.
- Last year of the Titleholders Championship, until it was brought back for one final year in 1972.

1967

PLAYER OF THE YEAR – Kathy Whitworth
LEADING MONEY WINNER – Kathy Whitworth $32,937

MAJOR WINNERS:

U.S. OPEN – Catherine Lacoste (a), Virginia Hot Springs G&TC (+10)
Runner(s) Up: Susie Berning, Beth Stone (+12)
LPGA – Kathy Whitworth, Pleasant Valley CC (-8)
Runner(s) Up: Shirley Englehorn (-7)
WESTERN OPEN – Kathy Whitworth, Pekin CC (-11)
Runner(s) Up: Sandra Haynie (-8)
ROOKIE OF THE YEAR – Sharron Moran
U.S. WOMEN'S AMATEUR – Mary Lou Dill, Annandale GC (5&4)
Runner Up: Jean Ashley

HIGHLIGHTS

- Last year of the Western Open as Major.
- Catherine Lacoste of France becomes the first amateur to win the U.S. Women's Open.

1968

PLAYER OF THE YEAR – Kathy Whitworth
LEADING MONEY WINNER – Kathy Whitworth $48,379

MAJOR WINNERS:

U.S. OPEN – Susie Berning, Moselem Springs GC (+5)
Runner(s) Up: Mickey Wright (+8)
LPGA – Sandra Post, Pleasant Valley CC (+2)
Runner(s) Up: Kathy Whitworth (+2)
ROOKIE OF THE YEAR – Sandra Post
U.S. WOMEN'S AMATEUR – JoAnne Carner, Birmingham CC (5&4)
Runner Up: Anne Sander

HIGHLIGHTS:

* Sandra Post wins the LPGA Championship by seven strokes in a playoff over Kathy Whitworth, 68-75.
* Both Kathy Whitworth and Carol Mann record ten wins on Tour.
* JoAnne Carner wins her 5th U.S. Amateur

1969

PLAYER OF THE YEAR – Kathy Whitworth
LEADING MONEY WINNER – Carol Mann $49,152

MAJOR WINNERS:

U.S. OPEN – Donna Caponi, Scenic Hills CC (+2)
Runner(s) Up: Peggy Wilson (+3)
LPGA – Betsy Rawls, Concord GC (+1)
Runner(s) Up: Carol Mann, Susie Berning (+5)
ROOKIE OF THE YEAR – Jane Blalock
U.S. WOMEN'S AMATEUR – Catherine Lacoste, Las Colinas CC (3&2)
Runner Up: Shelley Hamlin

HIGHLIGHTS

- JoAnne Carner becomes the first amateur to win an LPGA Tour event at the Burdine's Invitational

1970

PLAYER OF THE YEAR – Sandra Haynie
LEADING MONEY WINNER – Kathy Whitworth $30,235

MAJOR WINNERS:

U.S. OPEN – Donna Caponi, Muskogee CC (+3)
Runner(s) Up: Sandra Haynie, Sandra Spuzich (+4)
LPGA – Shirley Englehorn, Pleasant Valley CC (-7)
Runner(s) Up: Kathy Whitworth (-7)
ROOKIE OF THE YEAR – JoAnne Carner
U.S. WOMEN'S AMATEUR CHAMPION – Martha Wilkinson,
Wee Burn CC (3&2)
Runner Up: Cynthia Hill

HIGHLIGHTS

- LPGA great Mickey Wright retires from full-time competition.
- Shirley Englehorn records a 74 to Kathy Whitworth's 78 to win the LPGA championship in a playoff.

1971

PLAYER OF THE YEAR – Kathy Whitworth

LEADING MONEY WINNER – Kathy Whitworth $41,181

MAJOR WINNERS:

U.S. OPEN – JoAnne Carner, Kahkwa Club (E)

Runner(s) Up: Kathy Whitworth (+7)

LPGA – Kathy Whitworth, Pleasant Valley CC (-4)

Runner(s) Up: Kathy Ahern (E)

ROOKIE OF THE YEAR – Sally Little

U.S. WOMEN'S AMATEUR CHAMPION – Laura Baugh, Atlanta CC (1 up)

Runner Up: Beth Barry

HIGHLIGHTS

- JoAnne Carner becomes the first person ever to win three different USGA events. (U.S. Open, U.S. Women's Amateur, U.S. Girl's Junior Amateur).
- Laura Baugh wins the U.S. Amateur at age 16.

1972

PLAYER OF THE YEAR – Kathy Whitworth

LEADING MONEY WINNER – Kathy Whitworth $65,063

MAJOR WINNERS:

U.S. OPEN – Susie Berning, Winged Foot GC (+11)

Runner(s) Up: Kathy Ahern, Pam Barnett, Judy Rankin (+12)

LPGA – Kathy Ahern, Pleasant Valley CC (+1)

Runner(s) Up: Jane Blalock (+7)

TITLEHOLDERS – Sandra Palmer, Pine Needles L&GC (-1)

Runner(s) Up: Judy Rankin, Mickey Wright (+9)
ROOKIE OF THE YEAR – Jocelyne Bourassa
U.S. WOMEN'S AMATEUR CHAMPION – Mary Budke, St. Louis CC (5&4)
Runner Up: Cynthia Hill

HIGHLIGHTS
- Titleholders Championship was a featured major from 1937-1942, 1946-1966, and this year, 1972.
- LPGA player Jane Blalock is accused of cheating by improving her lie in several instances. This episode and the commotion to follow led to the establishment of the commissioner position.

1973

PLAYER OF THE YEAR – Kathy Whitworth
LEADING MONEY WINNER – Kathy Whitworth $82,864

MAJOR WINNERS:
U.S. OPEN – Susie Berning, CC of Rochester (+2)
Runner(s) Up: Shelley Hamlin, Gloria Ehret (+7)
LPGA – Mary Mills, Pleasant Valley CC (-4)
Runner(s) Up: Betty Burfeindt (-3)
ROOKIE OF THE YEAR – Laura Baugh
U.S. WOMEN'S AMATEUR CHAMPION – Carol Semple, Montclair GC (1 up)
Runner Up: Anne Sander

HIGHLIGHTS

- First year of the du Maurier classic, which would be played as a major championship from 1979-2000.
- Mickey Wright wins her 82nd and final tournament, putting her second all-time behind Kathy Whitworth's 88.

1974

PLAYER OF THE YEAR – JoAnne Carner
LEADING MONEY WINNER – JoAnne Carner $87,094

MAJOR WINNERS:

U.S. OPEN – Sandra Haynie, La Grange CC (+7)
Runner(s) Up: Beth Stone, Carol Mann (+8)
LPGA – Sandra Haynie, Pleasant Valley CC (-4)
Runner(s) Up: JoAnne Carner (-2)
ROOKIE OF THE YEAR – Jan Stephenson
U.S. WOMEN'S AMATEUR CHAMPION – Cynthia Hill, Broadmoor GC (5&4)
Runner Up: Carol Semple

HIGHLIGHTS

- Bonnie Bryant wins the LPGA Bill Branch Classic, becoming the first (and only) lefty golfer to win on the LPGA Tour.
- Sandra Haynie wins both majors.

1975

PLAYER OF THE YEAR – Sandra Palmer
LEADING MONEY WINNER – Sandra Palmer $76,374

MAJOR WINNERS:

U.S. OPEN – Sandra Palmer, Atlantic City CC (+7)
Runner(s) Up: JoAnne Carner, Sandra Post, Nancy Lopez (a) (+11)
LPGA – Kathy Whitworth, Pine Ridge GC (-4)
Runner(s) Up: Sandra Haynie (-3)
ROOKIE OF THE YEAR – Amy Alcott
U.S. WOMEN'S AMATEUR CHAMPION – Beth Daniel, Brae Burn CC (3&2)
Runner Up: Donna Horton

HIGHLIGHTS

- Amy Alcott records her first LPGA Tour victory at the age of 19.
- Lack of funds call for a tournament cancellation in Houston.

1976

PLAYER OF THE YEAR – Judy Rankin
LEADING MONEY WINNER – Judy Rankin $150,734

MAJOR WINNERS:

U.S. OPEN – JoAnne Carner, Rolling Green GC (+8)
Runner(s) Up: Sandra Palmer (+8)
LPGA – Betty Burfeindt, Pine Ridge GC (-5)
Runner(s) Up: Judy Rankin (-4)

ROOKIE OF THE YEAR – Bonnie Lauer

U.S. WOMEN'S AMATEUR CHAMPION – Donna Horton, Del Paso CC (2&1)

Runner Up: Marianne Bretton

HIGHLIGHTS

- First year in which a player accumulates over $100,000 in prize money, done by Judy Rankin with $150,734.
- The British Women's Open is played for the first time.

1977

PLAYER OF THE YEAR – Judy Rankin

LEADING MONEY WINNER – Judy Rankin $122,890

MAJOR WINNERS:

U.S. OPEN – Hollis Stacy, Hazeltine GC (+4)

Runner(s) Up: Nancy Lopez (+6)

LPGA – Chako Higuchi, Bay Tree Golf Plantation (-5)

Runner(s) Up: Pat Bradley, Sandra Post, Judy Rankin (-6)

ROOKIE OF THE YEAR – Debbie Massey

U.S. WOMEN'S AMATEUR CHAMPION – Beth Daniel, Cincinnati CC (3&1)

Runner Up: Cathy Sherk

HIGHLIGHTS

- Se Ri Pak, credited with putting Korean golf on the map, is born.
- Chako Higuchi became the first Japanese player to win an

LPGA major and is still the only player from Japan to have won an LPGA major.

1978

PLAYER OF THE YEAR – Nancy Lopez
LEADING MONEY WINNER – Nancy Lopez $189,814

MAJOR WINNERS:

U.S. OPEN – Hollis Stacy, CC of Indianapolis (+5)
Runner(s) Up: JoAnne Carner, Sally Little (+6)
LPGA – Nancy Lopez, Jack Nicklaus Sports Center (-13)
Runner(s) Up: Amy Alcott (-7)
ROOKIE OF THE YEAR – Nancy Lopez
U.S. WOMEN'S AMATEUR CHAMPION – Cathy Sherk, Sunnybrook GC (4&3)
Runner Up: Judith Oliver

HIGHLIGHTS

- Nancy Lopez accumulated nine wins, including five-in-a-row in one stretch in her rookie year, becoming both the rookie and player of the year.
- Hollis Stacy won the U.S. Women's Open for the second year in a row.

1979

PLAYER OF THE YEAR – Nancy Lopez
LEADING MONEY WINNER – Nancy Lopez $197,489

MAJOR WINNERS:

U.S. OPEN – Jerilyn Britz, Brooklawn CC (E)
Runner(s) Up: Debbie Massey, Sandra Palmer (+2)
DU MAURIER – Amy Alcott, Richelieu Valley GC (-7)
Runner(s) Up: Nancy Lopez (-4)
LPGA – Donna Caponi, Jack Nicklaus Sports Center (-9)
Runner(s) Up: Jerilyn Britz (-6)
ROOKIE OF THE YEAR – Beth Daniel
U.S. WOMEN'S AMATEUR CHAMPION – Carolyn Hill, Memphis CC (7&6)
Runner Up: Patty Sheehan

HIGHLIGHTS

- Mickey Wright plays her way into a playoff at the LPGA Coca-Cola Classic, nine years after her retirement from playing full time.
- Nancy Lopez wins eight times and attains the lowest scoring average on Tour along with Player of the Year.
- First year of the du Maurier Classic.

1980

PLAYER OF THE YEAR – Beth Daniel
LEADING MONEY WINNER – Beth Daniel $231,000

MAJOR WINNERS:

U.S. OPEN – Amy Alcott, Richland CC (-4)

Runner(s) Up: Hollis Stacy (+5)

DU MAURIER – Pat Bradley, St. George's G&CC (-15)

Runner(s) Up: JoAnne Carner (-14)

LPGA – Sally Little, Jack Nicklaus Sports Center (-3)

Runner(s) Up: Jane Blalock (E)

ROOKIE OF THE YEAR – Myra Blackwelder

U.S. WOMEN'S AMATEUR CHAMPION – Juli Inkster, Prairie Dunes CC (2 up)

Runner Up: Patti Rizzo

HIGHLIGHTS

- Nancy Lopez became the youngest player to win 20 events at just 23 years, 7 months, and 26 days old.
- Total prize money for the year was $5 million.

1981

PLAYER OF THE YEAR – JoAnne Carner

LEADING MONEY WINNER – Beth Daniel $206,998

MAJOR WINNERS:

U.S. OPEN – Pat Bradley, La Grange CC (-9)

Runner(s) Up: Beth Daniel (-8)

DU MAURIER – Jan Stephenson, Summerlea G&CC (-10)

Runner(s) Up: Pat Bradley, Nancy Lopez (-9)

LPGA – Donna Caponi, Jack Nicklaus Sports Center (-8)

Runner(s) Up: Jerilyn Britz, Pat Meyers (-7)

ROOKIE OF THE YEAR – Patty Sheehan
U.S. WOMEN'S AMATEUR CHAMPION – Juli Inkster, Waverly CC (1 up)
Runner Up: Lindy Goggin

HIGHLIGHTS

- Kathy Whitworth became the first LPGA player to make over $1 million in her career.
- Patty Sheehan began her professional career on a high note by winning rookie of the year.

1982

PLAYER OF THE YEAR – JoAnne Carner
LEADING MONEY WINNER – JoAnne Carner $310,400

MAJOR WINNERS:

U.S. OPEN – Janet Alex, Del Paso CC (-5)
Runner(s) Up: Beth Daniel, Donna White, JoAnne Carner, Sandra Haynie (+1)
DU MAURIER – Sandra Haynie, St. George's G&CC (-8)
Runner(s) Up: Beth Daniel (-7)
LPGA – Jan Stephenson, Jack Nicklaus Sports Center (-9)
Runner(s) Up: JoAnne Carner (-7)
ROOKIE OF THE YEAR – Patti Rizzo
U.S. WOMEN'S AMATEUR CHAMPION – Juli Inkster, Broadmoor GC (4&3)
Runner Up: Cathy Hanlon

HIGHLIGHTS

- Kathy Whitworth passed Mickey Wright with all-time wins when she won her 83rd LPGA tournament.
- LPGA Headquarters moved from New York to Texas.

1983

PLAYER OF THE YEAR – Patty Sheehan
LEADING MONEY WINNER – JoAnne Carner $291,404

MAJOR WINNERS:

NABISCO – Amy Alcott, Mission Hills CC (-6)
Runner(s) Up: Beth Daniel, Kathy Whitworth (-4)
U.S. OPEN – Jan Stephenson, Cedar Ridge CC (+6)
Runner(s) Up: JoAnne Carner, Patty Sheehan (+7)
DU MAURIER – Hollis Stacy, Beaconsfield GC (-11)
Runner(s) Up: JoAnne Carner, Alice Miller (-9)
LPGA – Patty Sheehan, Jack Nicklaus Sports Center (-9)
Runner(s) Up: Sandra Haynie (-7)
ROOKIE OF THE YEAR – Stephanie Farwig
U.S. WOMEN'S AMATEUR CHAMPION – Joanne Pacillo, Canoe Brook CC (2&1)
Runner Up: Sally Quinlan

HIGHLIGHTS

- First year that the Nabisco Dinah Shore became an LPGA major.
- Both Patty Sheehan and Pat Bradley recorded four wins this year, but Sheehan won a major.

1984

PLAYER OF THE YEAR – Betsy King
LEADING MONEY WINNER – Betsy King $266,771

MAJOR WINNERS:
NABISCO – Juli Inkster, Mission Hills CC (-8)
Runner(s) Up: Pat Bradley (-8)
U.S. OPEN – Hollis Stacy, Salem CC (+2)
Runner(s) Up: Rosie Jones (+3)
DU MAURIER – Juli Inkster, St. George's G&CC (-9)
Runner(s) Up: Ayako Okamoto (-8)
LPGA – Patty Sheehan, Jack Nicklaus Sports Center (-16)
Runner(s) Up: Pat Bradley, Beth Daniel (-6)
ROOKIE OF THE YEAR – Juli Inkster
U.S. WOMEN'S AMATEUR CHAMPION – Deb Richard, Broadmoor GC (37 holes)
Runner Up: Kimberly Williams

HIGHLIGHTS
- Juli Inkster made a par on the first sudden death playoff hole in the ANA Inspiration to clinch her first major win over Pat Bradley.
- This was Juli Inkster's rookie year, and she became the first rookie to win two majors as a rookie.
- Mary Beth Zimmerman set a new nine-hole record low in relation to par, an 8-under 28.

1985

PLAYER OF THE YEAR – Nancy Lopez
LEADING MONEY WINNER – Nancy Lopez $416,472

MAJOR WINNERS:

NABISCO – Alice Miller, Mission Hills CC (-13)
Runner(s) Up: Jan Stephenson (-10)
U.S. OPEN – Kathy Baker, Baltusrol GC (-8)
Runner(s) Up: Judy Clark (-5)
DU MAURIER – Pat Bradley, Beaconsfield GC (-10)
Runner(s) Up: Jane Geddes (-9)
LPGA – Nancy Lopez, Jack Nicklaus Sports Center (-15)
Runner(s) Up: Alice Miller (-7)
ROOKIE OF THE YEAR – Penny Hammel
U.S. WOMEN'S AMATEUR CHAMPION – Michiko Hattori, Fox Chapel CC (5&4)
Runner Up: Cheryl Stacy

HIGHLIGHTS

- Kathy Whitworth finished her record career with an 88th win at the United Virginia Bank Classic. This record still holds today.
- Alice Miller's first ever win was a major, the Nabisco Dinah Shore.

1986

PLAYER OF THE YEAR – Pat Bradley
LEADING MONEY WINNER – Pat Bradley $492,021

MAJOR WINNERS:

NABISCO – Pat Bradley, Mission Hills CC (-8)

Runner(s) Up: Val Skinner (-6)

U.S. OPEN – Jane Geddes, NRC CC (-1)

Runner(s) Up: Sally Little (-1)

DU MAURIER – Pat Bradley, Board of Trade CC (-12)

Runner(s) Up: Ayako Okamoto (-12)

LPGA – Pat Bradley, Jack Nicklaus Sports Center (-11)

Runner(s) Up: Patty Sheehan (-10)

ROOKIE OF THE YEAR – Jody Rosenthal

U.S. WOMEN'S AMATEUR CHAMPION – Kay Cockerill, Pasatiempo GC (9&7)

Runner Up: Kathleen McCarthy

HIGHLIGHTS

- Jane Geddes won the Women's U.S. Open by two in an 18-hole play-off against Sally Little after they tied at the end of regulation play.
- In the du Maurier Classic, Pat Bradley birdied the first sudden-death playoff hole to win over Ayako Okamoto.
- Pat Bradley would have completed a Grand Slam this year if she had won the Women's U.S. Open, but she finished in fifth place, just three strokes off the lead. She did, however, complete her career Grand Slam this year.

1987

PLAYER OF THE YEAR – Ayako Okamoto

LEADING MONEY WINNER – Ayako Okamoto $466,034

MAJOR WINNERS:

NABISCO – Betsy King, Mission Hills CC (-5)

Runner(s) Up: Patty Sheehan (-5)

U.S. OPEN – Laura Davies, Plainfield CC (-3)

Runner(s) Up: Ayako Okamoto, JoAnne Carner (-3)

DU MAURIER – Jody Rosenthal, Islesmere GC (-16)

Runner(s) Up: Ayako Okamoto (-14)

MAZDA LPGA – Jane Geddes, Jack Nicklaus Sports Center (-13)

Runner(s) Up: Betsy King (-12)

ROOKIE OF THE YEAR – Tammie Green

U.S. WOMEN'S AMATEUR CHAMPION – Kay Cockerill, Rhode Island CC (3&2)

Runner Up: Tracy Kerdyk

HIGHLIGHTS

- In the Nabisco, Betsy King won over Patty Sheehan on the second sudden-death playoff hole with a par.
- The U.S. Open playoff occurred over 18 holes between three players: Laura Davies, Ayako Okamoto, and JoAnne Carner. They finished at 1-under, 1-over, and 2-over, respectively.
- Pat Bradley became the first LPGA player to exceed $2 million in career winnings.

1988

PLAYER OF THE YEAR – Nancy Lopez

LEADING MONEY WINNER – Sherri Turner $350,851

MAJOR WINNERS:

NABISCO – Amy Alcott, Mission Hills CC (-14)

Runner(s) Up: Colleen Walker (-12)

U.S. OPEN – Liselotte Neumann, Baltimore CC (-7)

Runner(s) Up: Patty Sheehan (-4)

DU MAURIER – Sally Little, Vancouver GC (-9)

Runner(s) Up: Laura Davies (-8)

MAZDA LPGA – Sherri Turner, Jack Nicklaus Sports Center (-7)

Runner(s) Up: Amy Alcott (-6)

ROOKIE OF THE YEAR – Liselotte Neumann

U.S. WOMEN'S AMATEUR CHAMPION – Pearl Sinn, Minikahda Club (6&5)

Runner Up: Karen Noble

HIGHLIGHTS

- Liselotte Neumann won the Women's U.S. Open as a rookie, a feat that only few have ever accomplished.
- LPGA headquarters were moved, once again, from Texas to Daytona Beach, Florida.

1989

PLAYER OF THE YEAR – Betsy King

LEADING MONEY WINNER – Betsy King $654,132

MAJOR WINNERS:

NABISCO – Juli Inkster, Mission Hills CC (-9)

Runner(s) Up: JoAnne Carner, Tammie Green (-4)

U.S. OPEN – Betsy King, Indianwood G&CC (-6)

Runner(s) Up: Nancy Lopez (-2)

DU MAURIER – Tammie Green, Beaconsfield GC (-9)

Runner(s) Up: Pat Bradley, Betsy King (-8)

MAZDA LPGA – Nancy Lopez, Jack Nicklaus Sports Center (-14)

Runner(s) Up: Ayako Okamoto (-11)

ROOKIE OF THE YEAR – Pamela Wright

U.S. WOMEN'S AMATEUR CHAMPION – Vicki Goetze, Pinehurst CC (4&3)

Runner Up: Brandie Burton

HIGHLIGHTS

Betsy King won six tournaments.

LPGA tournament prize money totaled $14 million this year.

*Two young golfer programs were founded: LPGA-USGA Girls Golf and the LPGA Urban Youth Golf Program.

1990

PLAYER OF THE YEAR – Beth Daniel

LEADING MONEY WINNER – Beth Daniel $863,578

MAJOR WINNERS:

NABISCO – Betsy King, Mission Hills CC (-5)

Runner(s) Up: Shirley Furlong, Kathy Postlewait (-3)

U.S. OPEN – Betsy King, Atlantic Athletic Club (-4)

Runner(s) Up: Patty Sheehan (-3)

DU MAURIER – Cathy Johnston-Forbes, Westmount G&CC (-16)

Runner(s) Up: Patty Sheehan (-14)

MAZDA LPGA – Beth Daniel, Bethesda CC (-4)
Runner(s) Up: Rosie Jones (-3)
ROOKIE OF THE YEAR – Hiromi Kobayashi
U.S. WOMEN'S AMATEUR CHAMPION – Pat Hurst, Canoe
Brook CC (37 holes)
Runner Up: Stephanie Davis

HIGHLIGHTS

- The Mazda LPGA Championship was the first LPGA event to have a purse of $1 million.
- Beth Daniel won seven tournaments this year.
- The first Solheim Cup is held. The United States beat Europe 11 ½ to 4 ½.

1991

PLAYER OF THE YEAR – Pat Bradley
LEADING MONEY WINNER – Pat Bradley $763,118

MAJOR WINNERS:

NABISCO – Amy Alcott, Mission Hills CC (-15)
Runner(s) Up: Dottie Pepper (-7)
U.S. OPEN – Meg Mallon, Colonial CC (-1)
Runner(s) Up: Pat Bradley (+1)
DU MAURIER – Nancy Scranton, Vancouver GC (-9)
Runner(s) Up: Debbie Massey (-6)
MAZDA LPGA – Meg Mallon, Bethesda Country Club (-10)
Runner(s) Up: Pat Bradley, Ayako Okamoto (-9)

ROOKIE OF THE YEAR – Brandie Burton

U.S. WOMEN'S AMATEUR CHAMPION – Amy Fruhwirth, Prairie Dunes CC (5&4)

Runner Up: Heidi Voorhees

HIGHLIGHTS

- Pat Bradley won four events, but three of them came in one month, September.
- The LPGA had 21 unique winners, a new record.

1992

PLAYER OF THE YEAR – Dottie Pepper

LEADING MONEY WINNER – Dottie Pepper $693,335

MAJOR WINNERS:

NABISCO – Dottie Pepper, Mission Hills CC (-9)

Runner(s) Up: Juli Inkster (-9)

U.S. OPEN – Patty Sheehan, Oakmont CC (-4)

Runner(s) Up: Juli Inkster (-4)

DU MAURIER – Sherri Steinhauer, St. Charles CC (-11)

Runner(s) Up: Judy Dickinson (-9)

MAZDA LPGA – Betsy King, Bethesda Country Club (-17)

Runner(s) Up: Karen Noble, Liselotte Neumann, Joanne Carner (-6)

ROOKIE OF THE YEAR – Helen Alfredsson

U.S. WOMEN'S AMATEUR CHAMPION – Vicki Goetze, Kemper Lakes G.C. (1 up)

Runner Up: Annika Sorenstam

HIGHLIGHTS

- An 18-hole playoff decided the winner of the U.S. Women's Open this year, where Patty Sheehan defeated Juli Inkster by shooting a 72 (+1) to Inkster's 74 (+3).
- Shelly Hamlin returned to the LPGA after a mastectomy. She won the Phar-Mor golf tournament, her first win since 1978.
- The Susan G. Komen Breast Cancer Foundation became the official national charity of the LPGA.

1993

PLAYER OF THE YEAR – Betsy King
LEADING MONEY WINNER – Betsy King $595,992

MAJOR WINNERS:

NABISCO – Helen Alfredsson, Mission Hills CC (-4)
Runner(s) Up: Amy Benz, Tina Barrett, Betsy King (-2)
U.S. OPEN – Lauri Merten, Crooked Stick GC (-8)
Runner(s) Up: Donna Andrews, Helen Alfredsson (-7)
DU MAURIER – Brandie Burton, London Hunt Club (-11)
Runner(s) Up: Betsy King (-11)
MAZDA LPGA – Patty Sheehan, Bethesda Country Club (-9)
Runner(s) Up: Lauri Merten (-8)
ROOKIE OF THE YEAR – Suzanna Strudwick
U.S. WOMEN'S AMATEUR CHAMPION – Jill McGill, San Diego C.C. (1 up)
Runner Up: Sarah LeBrun

HIGHLIGHTS

- Brandie Burton only needed one sudden death playoff hole to win the du Maurier Classic. She birdied the hole to beat Betsy King.
- Patty Sheehan qualified for the LPGA Hall of Fame.
- Although Betsy King did not win a major this year, she dominated the LPGA money list, Player of the Year, and had the lowest stroke average (70.85).

1994

PLAYER OF THE YEAR – Beth Daniel
LEADING MONEY WINNER – Laura Davies $687,201

MAJOR WINNERS:

NABISCO – Donna Andrews, Mission Hills CC (-12)
Runner(s) Up: Laura Davies (-11)
U.S. OPEN – Patty Sheehan, Indianwood G&CC (-7)
Runner(s) Up: Tammie Green (-6)
DU MAURIER – Martha Nause, Ottawa Hunt & GC (-9)
Runner(s) Up: Michelle McGann (-8)
MCDONDALD'S LPGA – Laura Davies, DuPont Country Club (-5)
Runner(s) Up: Alice Ritzman (-2)
ROOKIE OF THE YEAR – Annika Sorenstam
U.S. WOMEN'S AMATEUR CHAMPION – Wendy Ward, The Homestead (2&1)
Runner Up: Jill McGill

HIGHLIGHTS

- This was Laura Davies' first year topping the money list.
- Beth Daniel performed the best, winning the most LPGA events (four), player of the year, and lowest scoring average (70.90).

1995

PLAYER OF THE YEAR – Annika Sorenstam
LEADING MONEY WINNER – Annika Sorenstam $666,533

MAJOR WINNERS:

NABISCO – Nanci Bowen, Mission Hills CC (-3)
Runner(s) Up: Susie Redman (-2)
U.S. OPEN – Annika Sorenstam, Broadmoor (-6)
Runner(s) Up: Meg Mallon (-1)
DU MAURIER – Jenny Lidback, Beaconsfield GC (-8)
Runner(s) Up: Liselotte Neumann (-7)
MCDONALD'S LPGA – Kelly Robbins, DuPont CC (-10)
Runner(s) Up: Laura Davies (-9)
ROOKIE OF THE YEAR – Pat Hurst
U.S. WOMEN'S AMATEUR CHAMPION – Kelli Kuehne, The Country Club (Brookline) (4&3)
Runner Up: Anne-Marie Knight

HIGHLIGHTS

- This was the first year that Annika Sorenstam made a name for herself. She won player of the year, topped the money list, had the lowest scoring average, and won her first U.S. Women's Open.

- There were two first and only major winners: Nanci Bowen, who won the Nabisco Dinah Shore, and Jenny Lidback, who topped the leaderboard at the du Maurier Classic.

1996

PLAYER OF THE YEAR – Laura Davies
LEADING MONEY WINNER – Karrie Webb $1,002,000

MAJOR WINNERS:

NABISCO – Patty Sheehan, Mission Hills CC (-7)
Runner(s) Up: Kelly Robbins, Meg Mallon, Annika Sorenstam (-6)
U.S. OPEN – Annika Sorenstam, Pine Needles Lodge (-8)
Runner(s) Up: Kris Tschetter (-2)
DU MAURIER – Laura Davies, Edmonton CC (-11)
Runner(s) Up: Nancy Lopez, Karrie Webb (-9)
MCDONALD'S LPGA – Laura Davies, DuPont Country Club (E)
Runner(s) Up: Julie Piers (+1)
ROOKIE OF THE YEAR – Karrie Webb
U.S. WOMEN'S AMATEUR CHAMPION – Kelli Kuehne, Firethorn GC (2&1)
Runner Up: Marisa Baena

HIGHLIGHTS

- Annika Sorenstam won her second U.S. Women's Open in a row.
- Betsy King qualified for the LPGA Hall of Fame.
- Karrie Webb became the first LPGA Tour player to win over $1,000,000 in a single season.

1997

PLAYER OF THE YEAR – Annika Sorenstam
LEADING MONEY WINNER – Annika Sorenstam $1,236,789

MAJOR WINNERS:
NABISCO – Betsy King, Mission Hills CC (-12)
Runner(s) Up: Kris Tschetter (-10)
U.S. OPEN – Alison Nicholas, Pumpkin Ridge (-10)
Runner(s) Up: Nancy Lopez (-9)
DU MAURIER – Colleen Walker, Glen Abbey GC (-14)
Runner(s) Up: Liselotte Neumann (-12)
MCDONALD'S LPGA – Christa Johnson, DuPont Country Club (-3)
Runner(s) Up: Leta Lindley (-3)
ROOKIE OF THE YEAR – Lisa Hackney
U.S. WOMEN'S AMATEUR CHAMPION – Silvia Cavalleri, Brae Burn CC (5&4)
Runner Up: Robin Burke

HIGHLIGHTS
- A new LPGA record for most consecutive wins of the same event was set by Laura Davies when she won the Standard Register PING event for the fourth year in a row.
- The LPGA Championship, at the time tabbed the McDonald's LPGA Championship, took two extra holes to reach a winner. Christa Johnson won her only major with a par on the second playoff hole after both her and her competitor, Leta Lindley, bogeyed the first playoff hole.

1998

PLAYER OF THE YEAR – Annika Sorenstam
LEADING MONEY WINNER – Annika Sorenstam $1,092,748

MAJOR WINNERS:

NABISCO – Pat Hurst, Mission Hills CC (-7)
Runner(s) Up: Helen Dobson (-6)
U.S. OPEN – Se Ri Pak, Blackwolf Run (+6)
Runner(s) Up: Jenny Chuasiriporn (a) (+6)
DU MAURIER – Brandie Burton, Essex G&CC (-18)
Runner(s) Up: Annika Sorenstam (-17)
MCDONALD'S LPGA – Se Ri Pak, DuPont Country Club (-11)
Runner(s) Up: Donna Andrews, Lisa Hall (-8)
ROOKIE OF THE YEAR – Se Ri Pak
U.S. WOMEN'S AMATEUR CHAMPION – Grace Park, Barton Hills CC (7&6)
Runner Up: Jenny Chuasiriporn

HIGHLIGHTS

- The U.S. Women's Open took an extra 20 holes to reach its conclusion. Se Ri Pak and amateur Jenny Chuasiriporn were still tied after their 18-hole playoff, so they went to sudden death holes, where Pak birdied the second playoff hole (#11) to defeat Chuasiriporn.
- Pak is known for making a name for Korean golfers, and she won two majors this year, which was also her rookie year.

1999

PLAYER OF THE YEAR – Karrie Webb
LEADING MONEY WINNER – Karrie Webb $1,591,959

MAJOR WINNERS:

NABISCO – Dottie Pepper, Mission Hills CC (-19)
Runner(s) Up: Meg Mallon (-13)
U.S. OPEN – Juli Inkster, Old Waverly (-16)
Runner(s) Up: Sherri Turner (-11)
DU MAURIER – Karrie Webb, Alberta G&CC (-11)
Runner(s) Up: Laura Davies, (-9)
MCDONALD'S LPGA – Juli Inkster, DuPont Country Club (-16)
Runner(s) Up: Liselotte Neumann (-12)
ROOKIE OF THE YEAR – Mi Hyun Kim
U.S. WOMEN'S AMATEUR CHAMPION – Dorothy Delasin,
Biltmore Forest CC (4&3)
Runner Up: Jimin Kang

HIGHLIGHTS

- Three well-known names in women's golf, Juli Inkster, Amy Alcott, and Beth Daniel, joined the best of the best as they qualified for the LPGA and World Golf Halls of Fame this year.
- Karrie Webb dominated this year, winning most of the end-of-year awards.

PLAYER OF THE YEAR – Karrie Webb

LEADING MONEY WINNER – Karrie Webb $1,876,853

MAJOR WINNERS:

NABISCO – Karrie Webb, Mission Hills CC (-14)

Runner(s) Up: Dottie Pepper (-4)

U.S. OPEN – Karrie Webb, The Merit Club (-6)

Runner(s) Up: Cristie Kerr, Meg Mallon (-1)

*DU MAURIER – Meg Mallon, Royal Ottawa GC (-6)

Runner(s) Up: Rosie Jones (-5)

MCDONALD'S LPGA – Juli Inkster, DuPont Country Club (-3)

Runner(s) Up: Stefania Croce (-3)

ROOKIE OF THE YEAR – Dorothy Delasin

U.S. WOMEN'S AMATEUR CHAMPION – Marcy Newton, Waverley CC (8&7)

Runner Up: Laura Myerscough

HIGHLIGHTS

- Nabisco Dinah Shore becomes the Nabisco Championship.
- *Last year that the du Maurier Classic was considered a major. It has also since been renamed the Canadian Women's Open.
- Juli Inkster was the first to successfully defend her LPGA Championship title since Patty Sheehan did in 1984. Inkster did so by making par on the second playoff hole, while Stefania Croce made bogey.

PLAYER OF THE YEAR – Annika Sorenstam

LEADING MONEY WINNER – Annika Sorenstam $2,105,868

MAJOR WINNERS:

NABISCO – Annika Sorenstam, Mission Hills CC (-7)

Runner(s) Up: Karrie Webb (-4)

U.S. OPEN – Karrie Webb, Pine Needles Lodge (-7)

Runner(s) Up: Se Ri Pak (+1)

BRITISH OPEN – Se Ri Pak, Sunningdale (-11)

Runner(s) Up: Mi Hyun Kim (-9)

MCDONALD'S LPGA – Karrie Webb, DuPont Country Club (-14)

Runner(s) Up: Laura Diaz (-12)

ROOKIE OF THE YEAR – Hee-Won Han

U.S. WOMEN'S AMATEUR CHAMPION – Meredith Duncan,
Flint Hills National GC (37 holes)

Runner Up: Nicole Perrot

HIGHLIGHTS

- Women's British Open replaced the du Maurier Classic as the fourth major.
- Sorenstam became the first LPGA player to break 60 when she shot a 59 in the second round of the Standard Register PING event in Phoenix. At this tournament, she also shot the lowest 72-hole score in relation to par on the LPGA Tour (65-59-69-68 for a total of 27 under par).
- Donna Caponi was inducted into the LPGA and World Golf Halls of Fame.

PLAYER OF THE YEAR – Annika Sorenstam
LEADING MONEY WINNER – Annika Sorenstam $2,863,904

MAJOR WINNERS:

NABISCO – Annika Sorenstam, Mission Hills CC (-8)
Runner(s) Up: Liselotte Neumann (-7)
U.S. OPEN – Juli Inkster, Prairie Dunes (-4)
Runner(s) Up: Annika Sorenstam (-2)
BRITISH OPEN – Karrie Webb, Turnberry (-15)
Runner(s) Up: Michelle Ellis, Paula Marti (-13)
MCDONALD'S LPGA – Se Ri Pak, DuPont Country Club (-5)
Runner(s) Up: Beth Daniel (-2)
ROOKIE OF THE YEAR – Beth Bauer
U.S. WOMEN'S AMATEUR CHAMPION – Becky Lucidi, Sleepy Hollow CC (3&2)
Runner Up: Brandi Jackson

HIGHLIGHTS

- Official name of the Nabisco Championship changed to the Kraft Nabisco Championship.
- Another impressive year for Sorenstam, recording 11 wins and winning all the year-end awards.
- Juli Inkster became the second oldest female to win the U.S. Women's Open at 42 years, 13 days.

PLAYER OF THE YEAR – Annika Sorenstam
LEADING MONEY WINNER – Annika Sorenstam $2,029,506

MAJOR WINNERS:

NABISCO – Patricia Meunier-Lebouc, Mission Hills CC (-7)
Runner(s) Up: Annika Sorenstam (-6)
U.S. OPEN – Hilary Lunke, Pumpkin Ridge (-1)
Runner(s) Up: Kelly Robbins, Angela Stanford (-1)
BRITISH OPEN – Annika Sorenstam, Royal Lytham & St. Annes (-10)
Runner(s) Up: Se Ri Pak (-9)
MCDONALD'S LPGA – Annika Sorenstam, DuPont Country Club (-6)
Runner(s) Up: Grace Park (-6)
ROOKIE OF THE YEAR – Lorena Ochoa
U.S. WOMEN'S AMATEUR CHAMPION – Virada Nirapath-
pongporn, Philadelphia CC (2&1)
Runner Up: Jane Park

HIGHLIGHTS

- At the LPGA Championship, Sorenstam won in a sudden death playoff by making a par over Grace Park's bogey.
- A three-way, 18-hole playoff decided the U.S. Women's Open, where Hilary Lunke beat her competitors with a 70 (-1) to the others' 71 (E) and 73 (+2).
- Beth Daniel became the oldest winner of an LPGA event when she won the Canadian Women's Open at 46 years, 8 months, and 29 days.
- Annika was inducted into the LPGA and World Golf Halls of Fame. She also shot a 54-hole record of 24-under par at the Mizuno Classic.

2004

PLAYER OF THE YEAR – Annika Sorenstam
LEADING MONEY WINNER – Annika Sorenstam $2,544,707

MAJOR WINNERS:

NABISCO – Grace Park, Mission Hills CC (-11)
Runner(s) Up: Aree Song (-10)
U.S. OPEN – Meg Mallon, The Orchards (-10)
Runner(s) Up: Annika Sorenstam (-8)
BRITISH OPEN – Karen Stupples, Sunningdale (-19)
Runner(s) Up: Rachel Hetherington (-14)
MCDONALD'S LPGA – Annika Sorenstam, DuPont Country Club (-13)
Runner(s) Up: Shi-Hyun Ahn (-10)
ROOKIE OF THE YEAR – Shi-Hyun Ahn
U.S. WOMEN'S AMATEUR CHAMPION –Jane Park, The Kahkwa Club (2 up)
Runner Up: Amanda McCurdy

HIGHLIGHTS

- Minea Blomqvist shot a record round at the Women's British Open. She shot a 62 in the third round, the lowest round ever in an LPGA major.
- Karen Stupples won her first major this year. This was made possible in part to her back-to-back eagles on the first two holes of her final round.

2005

PLAYER OF THE YEAR – Annika Sorenstam
LEADING MONEY WINNER – Annika Sorenstam $2,588,240

MAJOR WINNERS:

NABISCO – Annika Sorenstam, Mission Hills CC (-15)
Runner(s) Up: Rosie Jones (-7)
U.S. OPEN – Birdie Kim, Cherry Hills (+3)
Runner(s) Up: Brittany Lang (a), Morgan Pressel (a) (+5)
BRITISH OPEN – Jeong Jang, Royal Birkdale (-16)
Runner(s) Up: Sophie Gustafson (-12)
MCDONALD'S LPGA – Annika Sorenstam, Bulle Rock (-11)
Runner(s) Up: Michelle Wie (a) (-8)
ROOKIE OF THE YEAR – Paula Creamer
U.S. WOMEN'S AMATEUR CHAMPION – Morgan Pressel, Ansley GC (9&8)
Runner Up: Maru Martinez

HIGHLIGHTS

- Annika tied Nancy Lopez's record of most consecutive wins when she won the Kraft Nabisco this year. She also set the record for number of consecutive wins at the same tournament when she won the Mizuno Classic a fifth time in a row.
- Birdie Kim won the U.S. Women's Open by holing a bunker shot on the 72nd hole.
- Karrie Webb was inducted into the LPGA and World Golf Halls of Fame.

2006

PLAYER OF THE YEAR – Lorena Ochoa
LEADING MONEY WINNER – Lorena Ochoa $2,592,872

MAJOR WINNERS:

NABISCO – Karrie Webb, Mission Hills CC (-9)
Runner(s) Up: Lorena Ochoa (-9)
U.S. OPEN – Annika Sorenstam, Newport Country Club (E)
Runner(s) Up: Pat Hurst (E)
BRITISH OPEN – Sherri Steinhauer, Royal Lytham & St. Annes (-3)
Runner(s) Up: Cristie Kerr, Sophie Gustafson (-4)
MCDONALD'S LPGA – Se Ri Pak, Bulle Rock (-8)
Runner(s) Up: Karrie Webb (-8)
ROOKIE OF THE YEAR – Seon-Hwa Lee
U.S. WOMEN'S AMATEUR CHAMPION – Kimberly Kim, Pumpkin Ridge GC (1 up)
Runner Up: Katharina Schallenberg

HIGHLIGHTS

- Karrie Webb won her 7th major in dramatic fashion, holing a shot from 116 yards out to force a playoff. She would go on to win on the first sudden death hole with a birdie over Ochoa's par.
- Annika won the U.S. Women's Open by four strokes in the 18-hole playoff with a 70.
- At the LPGA Championship, Se Ri Pak put a 201-yard shot to just inches for a tap-in birdie on the first playoff hole. Webb failed to make her birdie to extend the playoff.

2007

PLAYER OF THE YEAR – Lorena Ochoa
LEADING MONEY WINNER – Lorena Ochoa $4,364,994

MAJOR WINNERS:

NABISCO – Morgan Pressel, Mission Hills CC (-3)
Runner(s) Up: Catriona Matthew, Brittany Lincicome, Suzann
Pettersen (-2)
U.S. OPEN – Cristie Kerr, Pine Needles Lodge (-5)
Runner(s) Up: Angela Park, Lorena Ochoa (-3)
BRITISH OPEN – Lorena Ochoa, St. Andrews (-5)
Runner(s) Up: Maria McBride, Jee Young Lee (-1)
MCDONALD'S LPGA – Suzann Pettersen, Bulle Rock (-14)
Runner(s) Up: Karrie Webb (-13)
ROOKIE OF THE YEAR – Angela Park
U.S. WOMEN'S AMATEUR CHAMPION – Maria Jose Uribe,
Crooked Stick GC (1 up)
Runner Up: Amanda Blumenherst

HIGHLIGHTS

- Se Ri Pak became the fourth LPGA player to win the same
  tournament a record five times when she won the Jamie Farr
  Owens Corning Classic. She joined the likes of Mickey Wright,
  Kathy Whitworth, and Annika Sorenstam. Pak also got inducted into the LPGA and World Golf Halls of Fame this year.
- Morgan Pressel became the youngest LPGA player to win a
  major at the time, being just 18 years, 10 months, and 9 days old.

2008

PLAYER OF THE YEAR – Lorena Ochoa
LEADING MONEY WINNER – Lorena Ochoa $2,763,193

MAJOR WINNERS:

NABISCO – Lorena Ochoa, Mission Hills CC (-11)
Runner(s) Up: Suzann Pettersen, Annika Sorenstam (-6)
U.S. OPEN – Inbee Park, Interlachen (-9)
Runner(s) Up: Helen Alfredsson (-5)
BRITISH OPEN – Jiyai Shin, Sunningdale (-18)
Runner(s) Up: Yani Tseng (-15)
MCDONALD'S LPGA – Yani Tseng, Bulle Rock (-12)
Runner(s) Up: Maria (Hjorth) McBride (-12)
ROOKIE OF THE YEAR – Yani Tseng
U.S. WOMEN'S AMATEUR CHAMPION – Amanda Blumenherst,
Eugene CC (2&1)
Runner Up: Azahara Munoz

HIGHLIGHTS

- Yani Tseng was just a 19-year-old rookie when she won the LPGA Championship. Tseng defeated Maria (Hjorth) McBride when she birdied the fourth playoff hole.
- The LPGA put the first ever professional golf drug testing policy in place.
- Annika Sorenstam stepped away from playing professional golf this year to focus on family and business.

2009

PLAYER OF THE YEAR – Lorena Ochoa
LEADING MONEY WINNER – Jiyai Shin $1,807,334

MAJOR WINNERS:

NABISCO – Brittany Lincicome, Mission Hills CC (-9)
Runner(s) Up: Cristie Kerr, Kristy McPherson (-8)
U.S. OPEN – Eun-Hee Ji, Saucon Valley (E)
Runner(s) Up: Candie Kung (+1)
BRITISH OPEN – Catriona Matthew, Royal Lytham & St. Annes (-3)
Runner(s) Up: Karrie Webb (E)
MCDONALD'S LPGA – Anna Nordqvist, Bulle Rock (-15)
Runner(s) Up: Lindsey Wright (-11)
ROOKIE OF THE YEAR – Jiyai Shin
U.S. WOMEN'S AMATEUR CHAMPION – Jennifer Song, Old Warson CC (3&1)
Runner Up: Jennifer Johnson

HIGHLIGHTS

- Catriona Matthew won the Women's British Open this year, just 11 weeks after giving birth. She was also the first Scot to win an LPGA major.
- Lorena Ochoa continued to dominate the Tour after Annika left, winning her fourth player of the year in a row.

PLAYER OF THE YEAR – Yani Tseng
LEADING MONEY WINNER – Na Yeon Choi $1,871,166

MAJOR WINNERS:
NABISCO – Yani Tseng, Mission Hills CC (-13)
Runner(s) Up: Suzann Pettersen (-12)
U.S. OPEN – Paula Creamer, Oakmont Country Club (-3)
Runner(s) Up: Na Yeon Choi, Suzann Pettersen (+1)
BRITISH OPEN – Yani Tseng, Royal Birkdale Golf Club (-11)
Runner(s) Up: Katherine Kirk (-10)
WEGMANS LPGA – Cristie Kerr, Locust Hill CC (-19)
Runner(s) Up: Song-Hee Kim (-7)
ROOKIE OF THE YEAR – Azahara Munoz
U.S. WOMEN'S AMATEUR CHAMPION – Danielle Kang, Charlotte CC (2&1)
Runner Up: Jessica Korda

HIGHLIGHTS
- The LPGA Championship changed names, going from the McDonald's LPGA Championship to the Wegman's LPGA Championship.
- There were 24 official events this year, which was ten less than the number of events they had just two years prior.

PLAYER OF THE YEAR – Yani Tseng
LEADING MONEY WINNER – Yani Tseng $2,921,713

MAJOR WINNERS:

NABISCO – Stacy Lewis, Mission Hills CC (-13)

Runner(s) Up: Yani Tseng (-10)

U.S. OPEN – So Yeon Ryu, The Broadmoor: East Course (-3)

Runner(s) Up: Hee Kyung Seo (-3)

BRITISH OPEN – Yani Tseng, Carnoustie Golf Links (-16)

Runner(s) Up: Brittany Lang (-12)

WEGMANS LPGA – Yani Tseng, Locust Hill Country Club (-19)

Runner(s) Up: Morgan Pressel (-9)

ROOKIE OF THE YEAR – Hee Kyung Seo

U.S. WOMEN'S AMATEUR CHAMPION – Danielle Kang, Rhode Island CC (6&5)

Runner Up: Moriya Jutanugarn

HIGHLIGHTS

- The U.S. Women's Open used the 3-hole aggregate format for the playoff that took place. So Yeon Ryu dominated her opponent, birdieing two of the three holes to win by three.
- Only 23 LPGA Tour events were held this year, the lowest it had been in almost 40 years.
- Yani Tseng's two major victories this year made her the youngest professional golfer (from either Tour) to win five majors at age 22.

2012

PLAYER OF THE YEAR – Stacy Lewis

LEADING MONEY WINNER – Inbee Park $2,287,080

MAJOR WINNERS:

NABISCO – Sun Young Yoo, Mission Hills CC (-9)

Runner(s) Up: I.K. Kim (-9)

U.S. OPEN – Na Yeon Choi, Blackwolf Run (-7)

Runner(s) Up: Amy Yang (-3)

BRITISH OPEN – Jiyai Shin, Royal Liverpool Golf Club (-9)

Runner(s) Up: Inbee Park (E)

WEGMANS LPGA – Shanshan Feng, Locust Hill Country Club (-6)

Runner(s) Up: Mika Miyazato, Stacy Lewis, Suzann Pettersen, Eun-Hee Ji (-4)

ROOKIE OF THE YEAR – So Yeon Ryu

U.S. WOMEN'S AMATEUR CHAMPION – Lydia Ko, The Country Club (3&1)

Runner Up: Jaye Marie Green

HIGHLIGHTS

- At the Kraft Nabisco Championship, it only took Sun Young Yoo one hole to defeat I.K. Kim in a playoff. She birdied the par-5 18th hole at Mission Hills CC to claim victory.
- Stacy Lewis won four tournaments this year, winning her the Player of the Year title.

2013

PLAYER OF THE YEAR – Inbee Park

LEADING MONEY WINNER – Inbee Park $2,456,619

MAJOR WINNERS:

NABISCO– Inbee Park, Mission Hills CC (-15)

Runner(s) Up: So Yeon Ryu (-11)

U.S. OPEN – Inbee Park, Sebonack GC (-8)

Runner(s) Up: I.K. Kim (-4)

BRITISH OPEN – Stacy Lewis, St. Andrews (-8)

Runner(s) Up: Hee Young Park, Na Yeon Choi (-6)

WEGMANS LPGA – Inbee Park, Locust Hill CC (-5)

Runner(s) Up: Catriona Matthew (-5)

EVIAN – Suzann Pettersen, Evian Resort GC (-10)

Runner(s) Up: Lydia Ko (a) (-8)

ROOKIE OF THE YEAR – Moriya Jutanugarn

U.S. WOMEN'S AMATEUR CHAMPION – Emma Talley, CC of Charleston (2&1)

Runner Up: Cindy Feng

HIGHLIGHTS

- At the Wegman's LPGA, 36 holes had to be played on Sunday due to a Thursday wash-out. As for Inbee Park and Catriona Matthew, they had to play 39 holes that day as they went to sudden death playoff holes. After the pair tied the first two holes with pars, Park with two putts to win, drained an 18-foot birdie putt to win it.
- Inbee Park won six events this year, three of which were majors.

2014

PLAYER OF THE YEAR – Stacy Lewis

LEADING MONEY WINNER – Stacy Lewis $2,539,039

MAJOR WINNERS:

NABISCO – Lexi Thompson, Mission Hills CC (-14)

Runner(s) Up: Michelle Wie (-11)

U.S. OPEN – Michelle Wie, Pinehurst No.2 (-2)

Runner(s) Up: Stacy Lewis (E)

BRITISH OPEN – Mo Martin, Royal Birkdale Golf Club (-1)

Runner(s) Up: Suzann Pettersen, Shanshan Feng (E)

WEGMANS LPGA – Inbee Park, Monroe Golf Club (-11)

Runner(s) Up: Brittany Lincicome (-11)

EVIAN – Hyo Joo Kim, Evian Resort Golf Club (-11)

Runner(s) Up: Karrie Webb (-10)

ROOKIE OF THE YEAR – Lydia Ko

U.S. WOMEN'S AMATEUR CHAMPION – Kristen Gillman, Nassau CC (2 up)

Runner Up: Brooke Mackenzie Henderson

HIGHLIGHTS

- Inbee Park won her second consecutive Wegman's LPGA Championship by saving a par on the first sudden death hole, number 18.
- The "Race to the CME Globe" was introduced where there was a season-long points race on the Tour, from which the top 72 players on the points list and other winners make it to the Tour Championship. The concept is very similar to the PGA Tour's FedEx Cup.

2015

PLAYER OF THE YEAR – Lydia Ko

LEADING MONEY WINNER – Lydia Ko $2,800,802

MAJOR WINNERS:

ANA INSPIRATION – Brittany Lincicome, Mission Hills CC (-9)

Runner(s) Up: Stacy Lewis (-9)

U.S. OPEN – In Gee Chun, Lancaster CC (-8)

Runner(s) Up: Amy Yang (-7)

BRITISH OPEN – Inbee Park, Turnberry (-12)

Runner(s) Up: Jin Young Ko (-9)

KPMG WOMEN'S PGA CHAMPIONSHIP – Inbee Park, Westchester CC (-19)

Runner(s) Up: Sei Young Kim (-14)

EVIAN – Lydia Ko, Evian Resort Golf Club (-16)

Runner(s) Up: Lexi Thompson (-10)

ROOKIE OF THE YEAR – Sei Young Kim

U.S. WOMEN'S AMATEUR CHAMPION – Hannah O'Sullivan, Portland GC (3&2)

Runner Up: Sierra Brooks

HIGHLIGHTS

- The Kraft Nabisco changed its name to the ANA Inspiration.
- At the ANA, Brittany Lincicome and Stacy Lewis faced off on hole 18 three extra times to reach a winner. Lincicome came out on top when she parred it for the third time, as Lewis made bogey.
- Lydia Ko, age 18 years, 4 months, and 20 days, became the youngest player to win a major and the Player of the Year award.

2016

PLAYER OF THE YEAR – Ariya Jutanugarn

LEADING MONEY WINNER – Ariya Jutanugarn $2,550,947

MAJOR WINNERS:

ANA INSPIRATION – Lydia Ko, Mission Hills CC (-12)

Runner(s) Up: Charley Hull, In Gee Chun (-11)

U.S. OPEN – Brittany Lang, CordeValle GC (-6)

Runner(s) Up: Anna Nordqvist (-6)

BRITISH OPEN – Ariya Jutanugarn, Woburn G&CC (-16)

Runner(s) Up: Mo Martin, Mirim Lee (-13)

KPMG WOMEN'S PGA CHAMPIONSHIP – Brooke Henderson, Sahalee CC (-6)

Runner(s) Up: Lydia Ko (-6)

EVIAN – In Gee Chun, Evian Resort Golf Club (-21)

Runner(s) Up: So Yeon Ryu, Sung Hyun Park (-17)

ROOKIE OF THE YEAR – In Gee Chun

U.S. WOMEN'S AMATEUR CHAMPION – Eun Jeong Seong, Rolling Green GC (1 Up)

Runner Up: Virginia Elena Carta

HIGHLIGHTS

- At just 18 years of age, Brooke Henderson defeated world number one, Lydia Ko, in a sudden death playoff at the KPMG Women's PGA Championship. She put her approach on the par 4, 18th hole, to less than three feet and made the putt to birdie it and win.

- A ruling that resulted in Anna Nordqvist receiving a two-stroke penalty was a big factor in her loss to Brittany Lang in a 3-hole playoff at the U.S. Women's Open.

PLAYER OF THE YEAR – Sung Hyun Park, So Yeon Ryu
LEADING MONEY WINNER – Sung Hyun Park $2,335,883

MAJOR WINNERS:

ANA INSPIRATION – So Yeon Ryu, Mission Hills CC (-14)
Runner(s) Up: Lexi Thompson (-14)
U.S. OPEN – Sung Hyun Park, Trump National GC (-11)
Runner(s) Up: Hye-Jin Choi (-9)
BRITISH OPEN – In-Kyung Kim, Royal Lytham & St. Annes GC (-18)
Runner(s) Up: Jodi Ewart Shadoff (-16)
KPMG WOMEN'S PGA CHAMPIONSHIP – Danielle Kang,
Olympia Fields CC (-13)
Runner(s) Up: Brooke Henderson (-12)
EVIAN – Anna Nordqvist, Evian Resort Golf Club (-9)
Runner(s) Up: Brittany Altomare (-9)
ROOKIE OF THE YEAR – Sung Hyun Park
U.S. WOMEN'S AMATEUR CHAMPION – Sophia Schubert,
San Diego CC (6&5)
Runner Up: Albane Valenzuela

HIGHLIGHTS

- In the ANA Inspiration, Lexi Thompson was assessed two 2-stroke penalties during her final round after a viewer sent in footage showing how she failed to properly replace her ball on the green during the third round. After she received the news on the 13th tee, she moved to two shots behind the lead, but rallied back to force a playoff where she would fall to So Yeon Ryu, who birdied the first playoff hole. Both tours no longer allow viewers to send in video footage.

Chapter 12:
TRIVIA QUIZ

1. Who invented golf?
2. What were the first golf balls made from?
3. What is the origin of the term caddie?
4. What was the first trophy in THE OPEN?
5. When was the Claret Jug first presented to the winner of THE OPEN?
6. What is the official name of the Claret Jug?
7. What is the original meaning of fairway?
8. When was the stymie abolished?
9. What was the gutta-percha ball made from?
10. When were dimples added to golf balls?
11. What was the original name of the 9-iron?
12. What year were grooves first made on club faces?
13. What year were the first rules of golf published?
14. In what year did 18 holes become the standard?
15. What year was the first Golf Club in the U.S. formed?
16. In what year was the first formal women's golf tournament held?
17. What year was the first OPEN played?
18. What year was the USGA formed?
19. Where was the first OPEN Championship?
20. Who was first US citizen to win the British Amateur?
21. What year had the first sub-par round in the U.S. OPEN?
22. In what year did the Ryder Cup begin?
23. In 1929, how many strokes did Bobby Jones win the U.S. OPEN playoff by?
24. Who was the only person to win all four "majors" in the same year?
25. Who purchased the land for Augusta National?

26. What was the "shot heard around the world?"

27. In 1938, which rule was implemented?

28. During the second World War, the price of what rose dramatically?

29. What year was the first U.S. Women's Open held?

30. What year did the Green Jacket become a staple at The Masters?

31. What year was the LPGA founded?

32. Which major could Ben Hogan not compete in to attempt to complete a single-year Grand Slam?

33. In what year did the PGA Championship become stroke play?

34. In what event did the "greatest act of sportsmanship in history" occur (year and event)?

35. Which Jack Nicklaus golf course was the first "target golf" course?

36. How many majors has Jack Nicklaus won (a record)?

37. What year did the "Norman Slam" occur in?

38. How many strokes did Tiger Woods win his first major by?

39. What year did the World Golf Championships (WGC) series of events begin?

40. During which years did Tiger Woods complete what is called the "Tiger Slam?"

41. What did Jim Furyk accomplish in the final round of the Travelers Championship in 2016?

42. How many majors did Sergio Garcia play in before achieving his first win in a major?

43. How many penalty strokes did Mickey Wright suffer because of an extra club in her bag at the 1957 LPGA Tampa Women's Open?

44. How many Tour wins did Kathy Whitworth achieve (a record)?

45. What year was the first British Women's Open held (not as a major)?

46. What year was the first Solheim Cup held, and who won?

47. In what year did the Women's British Open become a major?

48. Who was the first LPGA golfer to break 60, and in what year did it occur?

49. Who is the oldest winner of an LPGA event?

50. Who won the Evian Masters to become the youngest LPGA major winner?

Chapter 13:
ACKNOWLEDGEMENTS

CRISTINE LONNSTROM – My wife and lifelong partner. Her many ideas and suggestions have greatly enhanced the quality of this book. She edited and read many drafts, as well as suggested topics to be researched. In addition, she is fun to play golf with.

SARA RISO – Siena student and CURCA Summer Scholar. She did a great deal of research for this book which was not easy going back to 1200 or so. She wrote sections, read and re-read drafts, made edits, made suggestions that improved the quality of the book, and helped to organize the entire book. Her input and effort were invaluable. I am deeply indebted to her.

SCOTT LAWYER – IT wizard at Siena College. Without his help this book would still be on the practice tee.

ALEC ODNOHA – Siena student and CURCA Summer Scholar. Alec made many substantial contributions to this book in its early stages.

DAVID BARRELL – Longtime friend and golf partner. Dave made many suggestions and edits that have made this a better book.

DR. FRED DECASPERIS – Siena colleague, longtime friend and golf partner. His suggestions and edits greatly improved the book.

DAVID SMITH – Vice President of Development for Siena College. His advice and suggestions regarding creation, production and marketing were invaluable.

CHARLES AND JOANNE RISO – The parents of Sara and we thank them for sending their wonderful daughter to Siena.

BY SARA

DR. LONNSTROM – For allowing me to take part in this project and guiding me along the way. I never thought my name would appear in a published book, but here I am. I am so grateful for such an amazing opportunity.

MY PARENTS (mentioned above) – For fostering my love for golf and supporting me along the way. The sacrifices they made and continue to make have not gone unnoticed. My role in this book would not have existed if not for them.

DAVE WRONOWSKI – My college coach at Siena College. He helped me through all the highs and lows that is college golf. I could not have asked for a better coach to guide me through this part of my golf career.

ABOUT THE AUTHORS

Dr. Douglas Lonnstrom, is a Professor of Statistics at Siena College for over 40 years. He is a golf historian who has written two golf history books, given numerous lectures on the history of golf, and has hosted a golf television show for five years. Lonnstrom is a member of The Golf Writers Association of America and The Golf Travel Writers Association.

Sara Riso is a current student at Siena College. She is pursuing a Bachelor of Science in Actuarial Science. Riso has always been around golf because of her family, but did not take to the game till she was about 11 years old. Riso has played in competitive tournaments, and her talent progressed every single year. She is a member and co-captain of the Division I golf team at Siena College. July 2017, she placed 4th in the New York State Women's Amateur. During the fall of 2017, she also won the 2017 Dartmouth Invitational.

CPSIA information can be obtained
at www.ICGtesting.com
Printed in the USA
BVHW041229121218
535331BV00019BA/648/P